D0065209

Making Sense of Attention Deficit/Hyperactivity Disorder

Making Sense of
Attention Deficit/Hyperactivity
Disorder

❁

Carol R. Lensch

Bergin & Garvey
Westport, Connecticut • London

Library of Congress Cataloging-in-Publication Data

Lensch, Carol R., 1949–
    Making sense of attention deficit/hyperactivity disorder / Carol
R. Lensch.
      p. cm.
    Includes bibliographical references and index.
    ISBN 0–89789–700–5 (alk. paper)
    1. Attention-deficit hyperactivity disorder. I. Title.
RJ506.H9L46 2000
616.85'89—dc21   99–36508

British Library Cataloguing in Publication Data is available.

Library of Congress Catalog Card Number: 99–36508
ISBN: 0–89789–700–5

First published in 2000

Bergin & Garvey, 88 Post Road West, Westport, CT 06881
An imprint of Greenwood Publishing Group, Inc.
www.greenwood.com

Printed in the United States of America

(∞)™

The paper used in this book complies with the
Permanent Paper Standard issued by the National
Information Standards Organization (Z39.48–1984).

10 9 8 7 6 5 4 3 2 1

dedicated
to all of the children who have blessed my life over the years

Contents

Preface

In recent years there has been a notable increase in the number of students being identified with Attention Deficit/Hyperactivity Disorder (AD/HD) in American schools. Although there is a tremendous amount of research being done in the area of AD/HD, parents, educators, and individuals with AD/HD are ill equipped to deal with the demands of the disorder. Only through extensive research and a better understanding of what AD/HD is can we expect to develop more effective means of dealing with AD/HD on a daily basis at home and in school.

The primary purpose of *Making Sense of Attention Deficit/Hyperactivity Disorder* is to bridge the gap between research knowledge and the knowledge in use by educators on AD/HD. The book is a review and interpretation of selected studies on the causes, co-occurrence with other disorders, diagnosis, and treatments of AD/HD. It provides the reader with the opportunity to gain an understanding of AD/HD for making mindful, informed decisions on approaches best suited to meet the challenges presented by this disorder.

Chapter 1 provides an overview of the book, as well as my purpose in writing the book. Five misconceptions are identified and refuted by research presented in Chapters 2 through 5. The findings of these studies lend support to: (1) a genetic and environmental basis for AD/HD; (2) a comorbid and heterogeneous nature to the disorder; (3) a need for educators to approach AD/HD from an educational perspective; (4) the need to consider a variety of interventions in addition to medication for the treatment of AD/HD; and (5) the unique response to interventions by individuals with AD/HD.

In conclusion, educators are seeking information on this disorder because they are faced with an ever-increasing number of students with AD/HD, and they want to meet effectively the needs of this growing population of children. The emphasis in Chapter 6 is on using a collaborative team approach, involving all people who have an impact on the life of a student with AD/HD. Only through knowledge, understanding, and collaboration can educators be empowered to do the job that so desperately needs to be done.

Acknowledgments

Acknowledgments are due to all those whose inspiration, encouragement, and feedback carried me through the process of writing this book. Thank you to my friends, mentors, and guides at Virginia Polytechnic Institute and State University—David Parks, Ph.D., Jerome Niles, Ed.D., Dianne Yardley, Ph.D., Patricia Kelly, Ed.D., as well as Carol Whittaker, Ed.D., director of Pupil Personnel Services with Roanoke County Schools, and Kay Longley, Ed.D., psychologist with Botetourt County Schools.

I appreciate the tireless efforts of those who reviewed and edited my book chapter by chapter, including Joan Dowdy, Lauren Beck, Sybil Taylor, Brenda East, Dayl Graves, and my dear friend, Pat Watson. Special thanks to my sister, Gail Higgins-Brush, N.P., for all of her help and for always being there for me, and to my daughter-in-law, Hendree Jones, Ph.D., researcher and instructor at Johns Hopkins University, for technical and moral support.

I especially want to thank my family for supporting and lovingly putting up with me during my research and writing. My children, Erik, Laurien, Carrie, and Kristi, have been my best teachers on my journey through life. My mother, Beatrice Ingerling, has always encouraged me to pursue my dreams. Last, but far from least, I want to express my appreciation to my husband, John Lensch, for his willingness to read endless drafts, give helpful suggestions, and patiently stand by me.

The writing of this book was truly a group effort and one that would have been difficult if not impossible to have done without the support and encouragement of others. Thank you all.

Abbreviations

ADD	Attention Deficit Disorder
AD/HD	Attention Deficit/Hyperactivity Disorder
AFF	Affective Disorders
APA	American Psychiatric Association
ATS	Attention Training System
BD	Behavioral Disorder
CD	Conduct Disorder
CPT	continuous performance task
DSM	*Diagnostic and Statistical Manual of Mental Disorders* (various editions)
EEG	electroencephalogram
EFA	essential fatty acid
FFA	free fatty acid
fMRI	functional magnetic resonance imaging
LBW	low-birth-weight
LD	Learning Disabled, Learning Disabilities
MRI	magnetic resonance imaging
NBW	normal-birth-weight
ODD	Oppositional Defiant Disorder
OHI	Other Health Impaired
PET	positron-emission tomography

SAICA	Social Adjustment Inventory for Children and Adolescents
SES	socioeconomic status
UADD	undifferentiated Attention Deficit Disorder
WISC-R	Wechsler Intelligence Scale for Children–Revised

---------------------------   1   ---------------------------

Introduction

The essential thing at the start is the habit of thinking.
—Henry Cabot Lodge

The study of how the human brain works, especially that of children, can
be both intriguing and challenging as one attempts to analyze how learning
takes place. As a special educator I have had an abundance of opportunities
to observe children, particularly those with special needs. Although our
educational system categorizes students into groups of special education
and general education, all children are special and unique in the ways in
which they learn. An area of particular interest and concern regarding individual learning differences is that of Attention Deficit/Hyperactivity Disorder (AD/HD). Typically, an AD/HD child will exhibit excessive motor
activity, impulsivity, and difficulty attending to tasks (American Psychiatric
Association [hereafter APA], 1994).

BACKGROUND

Over the years I have seen a growing number of students diagnosed as
having AD/HD. Between the years 1990 and 1995, the diagnosis of AD/HD
has more than doubled (Turecki, 1997). This increase in identification leads
one to question what changes have taken place to bring it about and what
can be done to deal with the challenges created by the increase and numbers
of children with the disorder. Has the nature of the student or the tolerance
of educators changed in recent years? Are there environmental or societal
factors to consider? The incidence of AD/HD is estimated to be 3–5% of

school-age children to as high as 12% depending on how the disorder is defined (Augustine & Damico, 1995; Patel, 1996).

The *Diagnostic and Statistical Manual of Mental Disorders*, fourth edition (*DSM-IV*) provides a detailed description of the characteristics that must be identified for a medical diagnosis of AD/HD (APA, 1994) (see Appendix A). These criteria are based on the observation of behavior and are divided into three subtypes: (1) Attention Deficit/Hyperactivity Disorder, Predominantly Hyperactive-Impulsive Type; (2) Attention Deficit/ Hyperactivity Disorder, Predominantly Inattentive Type; and (3) Attention Deficit/Hyperactivity Disorder, Combined Type. Previous editions have delineated between Attention Deficit Disorder (ADD) and AD/HD, but in keeping with the language and definition of subtypes used in *DSM-IV*, AD/HD will be used throughout this book.

The *DSM* has been revised and is now in its fourth edition. Have the criteria changed significantly? Perhaps the increase in the number of students being diagnosed with AD/HD is in part due to this inconsistency in defining the disorder. Or do we truly have more individuals with AD/HD in modern American society?

While some may believe that AD/HD is on the rise, other authorities contend that a pseudo AD/HD accounts for 50–60% of the diagnosed cases (Hallowell & Ratey, 1994). By pseudo AD/HD Hallowell and Ratey mean the manifestation of a set of behaviors that mimic AD/HD but are actually the result of environmental influences such as fast food, fast-paced media and video games, and a pervasive societal attitude toward immediate gratification.

It is my belief that more physiologically based diagnostic procedures must be developed and used to identify individuals with AD/HD. Technology is being developed that can accomplish this task through a clinical, scientific approach, including magnetic resonance imaging (MRI) (Castellanos et al., 1996) and positron-emission tomography (PET) (Weiss, 1990) by identifying brain differences. Currently, these techniques are used in research settings, but as they are proven and perfected they may become part of a routine diagnostic assessment.

AD/HD is also, in part, identified through the use of teacher-rating scales, and rater reliability is a factor. Behavioral-rating scales are very subjective and depend on the rater's tolerance and interpretation of student behavior. The use of computer software designed to diagnose AD/HD on the basis of an individual's performance on specific tasks is one way to remove rater bias.

Pediatricians, psychologists, and other child-care professionals have limited explanation for AD/HD. The etiology or cause(s) of AD/HD is unknown at this time. There are those who believe that AD/HD is genetically transmitted but are unable to prove that conclusively (Biederman & Faraone, 1996). Some studies show that there is a 30–80% chance that a child of an AD/HD parent will be AD/HD (Hallowell & Ratey, 1994). Others are studying fatty acid metabolism as a causal factor in AD/HD (Stevens et al., 1995). Joseph Biederman and Stephen Faraone (1996) have done extensive research on AD/HD with their findings leading them to conclude "that AD/HD is familial, and that AD/HD is associated with environmental adversity and social disability" (p.1). In spite of the research that is going on, there is no definitive proof as to the cause or causes of this potentially handicapping condition. An analysis and synthesis of the research is needed to make sense of the findings of the studies being done.

The apparent increase in the prevalence of AD/HD and the lack of a viable explanation for this phenomenon create a need for developing reasonable explanations as to the cause(s) of AD/HD. It is quite possible and, in fact, reasonable to expect that multiple causes may exist. In a quest to find answers to the many questions surrounding the cause(s) and diagnosis of AD/HD, taking a microscopic view seems in order. After all, studying this neurological disorder from a global, behavioral perspective has not yielded the results one would hope to attain.

THE DECADE OF THE BRAIN

The 1990s have been declared "The Decade of the Brain" (National Institutes of Health, 1994). During this decade there has been an abundance of research conducted on how the human brain functions. This is of particular interest to educators who recognize the brain as the ultimate center of learning. Brain research findings give credibility to what have been previously considered the "soft" studies of educational research (Viadero, 1996). We are now seeing a number of educational professionals and scholars synthesizing, presenting, and making connections between brain research and educational applications.

One educator who is drawing connections and expanding upon current brain theory is Robert Sylwester, author of *A Celebration of Neurons: An Educator's Guide to the Human Brain* (1995). As the title indicates, the book is written to bridge the gap between brain research and education. Sylwester believes educators are on the verge of a major professional transformation:

The education profession is now approaching a crossroads. We can continue to focus our energies on the careful observation of external behavior—a course that may be adequate for managing relatively mild learning disorders—or we can join the search for a scientific understanding of the brain mechanisms, processes, and malfunctions that affect the successful completion of complex learning tasks. (p.4)

Sylwester (1995) makes an analogy between medicine and education. He portrays both as having their beginnings on an operational level based solely on observation and intuition, or as he calls it, "professional folklore" (p.4). Medicine grew out of this model as a result of the application of scientific research and discovery. Education is now at the point of legitimizing itself by the same means. When I heard Sylwester speak at the Association for Supervision and Curriculum Development Conference in Williamsburg in December 1996, I could not help but get excited about the ideas that were incubating in my mind, not only because of what he said but also because he is an *educator* and not a neuroscientist. Maybe it was not so out of line for me to look at the brain and causes for AD/HD from an educator's perspective. He was suggesting a way to study learning "through the scientific understanding of brain mechanisms" (p.4) rather than through the observation of behaviors, as previously has been done.

As a species, we have moved away from reliance on our basic instincts. In more primitive times people had to rely on themselves for survival. As a result of modern conveniences and technology, our lives have changed drastically over the years. We have given up our self-reliance and developed a dependency on experts. A first course of action for most people in Western cultures when faced with a challenge is to run to someone perceived as having the answer, or the fix, for the problem. There are times when the expertise of a specialist is warranted, but we have given up the ownership of our own destiny by never developing our inner resources. Through reconnecting with our innerselves we can take back our inalienable right to our own lives. It is only through informed decision making that we can strive to become all that we are capable of being. We need to empower ourselves through knowledge and become experts in our own right.

Howard Gardner (1991) identifies three types of learners, and we may all fit within each of these at various points in our lives. The first is the *intuitive learner*, which is typically the young child with a naive set of beliefs based on concrete observations. The second, the *traditional student*, is the type successful at complying with all the rules and mastering the lessons taught within the school setting. The *disciplinary expert*, the third category, is the individual who can put it all together and through a mastery of the discipline is able to transfer and apply knowledge across settings. We are all capable of becoming disciplinary experts. Gardner says,

These individuals have sought to establish concepts and practices that provide the best possible account of the world in which we live, even when that account flies in the face of long-standing intuitions, received wisdom, or unwitting but well-entrenched stupidity. Instead of accepting the earth as flat, they have—in the spirit of Christopher Columbus—amassed evidence that it is spherical in shape. (p.11)

We all must become informed and thus empowered to make good decisions based on the evidence that neuroscientists have amassed on AD/HD. Above all, I want the reader to leave this experience with a greater understanding of AD/HD and thereby a sense of empowerment that will enable the reader to make a difference in the lives of those with AD/HD that he or she touches.

PURPOSE AND FORMAT

The purpose of this book is to provide a review of research relevant to AD/HD as a useful guide to educators in bridging the gap between research and practice. The term "educator" is being used in the broadest sense, intended to include all those who participate in the lives of children with AD/HD. I attempt to make sense of the research findings and draw connections among otherwise isolated studies. This book is not designed to give answers to all the questions associated with AD/HD, but rather to facilitate decision making through providing information on current research in the field. It is my contention that through a review of the research, practitioners and parents will be able to draw their own conclusions about the etiology, diagnosis, and treatment of AD/HD. In the final analysis these are the topics that are most salient to those of us who live and work with individuals with AD/HD.

For a long time I have been puzzled by the riddle of AD/HD. Through extensive reading on the subject I developed a conceptual map of the basic areas of research currently being done, as well as an historical framework of previous research. Patterns emerged that served as the basis for the format of this book.

The first step toward developing an understanding of AD/HD should be determining its origin. Therefore, the causes are the subject addressed in Chapter 2. It became apparent to me that this disorder is more complex than any one cause or definition implies. This logically led to the next step, the study of comorbidity (co-occurrence) of AD/HD with other disorders, which is the focus of Chapter 3.

Diagnosis is discussed in Chapter 4 to aid teachers in the understanding of the identification procedures used with AD/HD and comorbid disorders. Although educators do not make the medical diagnosis of AD/HD, they are often involved in the process. Intervention is probably the area most relevant to teachers as it has direct application to the classroom. Chapter 5 is a review of some effective practices for use by teachers with students with AD/HD.

In Chapter 6, I have come full circle, returning to some of the basic questions that have influenced the format of this book. Chapters 2 through 5 each grew out of a quest to find answers to the riddle of AD/HD. Misconceptions have developed regarding the cause(s), complexity, diagnosis, and treatment of the disorder. It seems fitting that at the end of our journey through a review of research on these topics I attempt to dispel the misconceptions. In this final chapter I try to make sense of the research in a way that I hope is useful to educators. To aid the educator in applying this information to meaningful practice, suggestions are given for working together collaboratively in learning communities. The roles of the team members are defined in terms of their relationship to one another.

ARTICLE SELECTION AND ORGANIZATION

There is a wealth of research being done on AD/HD. To narrow the selection I chose articles from journals that referee (review by experts) submissions before approving them for publication (see Appendix B). To locate articles, I conducted library and Internet searches; scanned reference lists in books and articles; attended conferences where experts presented papers on their research findings; and reviewed articles and books suggested by colleagues and friends. Through the use of a large matrix, I categorized the articles by topic, and this resulted in the formation of the chapters.

Next, I evaluated the articles for relevancy to educators. I defined relevancy as contributing to a basic understanding of AD/HD to enhance communication with parents and other professionals and to facilitate decision making, and also as having a direct application to teaching children with the disorder. A panel of readers was formed to provide feedback on the relevancy and readability of each chapter.

Each article was evaluated in terms of the research cited by the authors and whether the study supported and reflected the general findings of the literature. I carefully reviewed each article to see if the authors cited other researchers who were reputable. After having read many studies and books on the subject of AD/HD, I have become familiar with the names and work of many researchers in the field. Next, I evaluated each study to determine if the authors' findings were supported by the findings of the researchers they cited. I felt that it was important that the studies I reviewed reflect a broad, well-established body of literature.

Once I put each chapter together, I sent copies to my panel of readers, which consisted of an elementary school principal, a middle-school English teacher, and a high-school special education teacher. Based on their comments, I made revisions and added anecdotes. There are places throughout the book where I have used italics to distinguish my words from the words of those whom I was citing. A child psychiatrist who has expertise in the area of AD/HD reviewed Chapters 2 through 4 and provided feedback.

Chapter 5 has been approached differently due to the fact that there are a number of older interventions that have been well researched. Therefore, the categories of established techniques are reviewed and current research is cited where it contributes to the existing body of knowledge. The educational interventions are presented, for the most part, in chronological order to represent the evolutionary development of these interventions.

The articles included in this book have been selected to (1) stimulate thinking on the subject of AD/HD; (2) provide an indication of the trends in current research; (3) correct misconceptions about the disorder; (4) facilitate mindful decision making on the part of educators; and (5) enable educators to communicate knowledgeably with parents and other professionals regarding AD/HD.

The conceptualization of AD/HD is evolving. Although a great deal of research has been conducted in the area of AD/HD over the years, there has not been a consistent definition of the disorder (Barkley, 1990). For that reason some of the findings may be contradictory at this stage of development. Researchers can only report the results as they emerge, and the confusion will probably continue until there is a greater understanding of AD/HD. As with any scientific endeavor, much trial and error will no doubt precede illumination about the mechanisms at work in AD/HD.

Whenever research involves human subjects there are constraints on the nature of the studies that can be conducted. The majority of research related to AD/HD has been nonexperimental and therefore limited in the generalizations that can be made from the findings. In Appendix B, each study is identified as nonexperimental, quasi-experimental, and experimental to give the reader an indication of the types of studies being conducted and included for review. Definitions for nonexperimental, quasi-experimental, and experimental are provided in Appendix B. In addition, there are notations for studies that fall in other categories, including meta-analysis, systematic search of the literature, review of the literature, ethnography, and case studies.

REFERENCES

American Psychiatric Association (APA). (1994). *Diagnostic and statistical manual of mental disorders* (4th ed.). Washington, DC: Author.

Augustine, L., & Damico, J. (1995). Attention Deficit Hyperactivity Disorder: The scope of the problem. *Seminars in Speech and Language, 16*(4), 243–257.

Barkley, R. A. (1990). *Attention-Deficit Hyperactivity Disorder: A handbook for diagnosis and treatment.* New York: Guilford Press.

Biederman, J., & Faraone, S. (1996, Winter). On the brain: Studies on Attention Deficit Disorder. *The Harvard Mahoney Neuroscience Newsletter* [On-line], 5. Available: PsycINFO.

Castellanos, F. X., Giedd, J. N., Marsh, W. L., Hamburger, S. D., Vaituzis, A. C., Dickstein, D. P., Sarfatti, S., Vauss, Y., Snell, J., Lange, N., Kaysen, D., Krain, A. L., Ritchie, G. F., Rajapakse, J. C., & Rapoport, J. L. (1996). Quantitative brain magnetic resonance imaging in Attention Deficit Hyperactivity Disorder. *Archives of General Psychiatry, 53*, 607–616.

Gardner, H. (1991). *The unschooled mind.* New York: Basic Books.

Hallowell, E., & Ratey, J. (1994). *Driven to distraction.* New York: Random House.

National Institutes of Health. (1994). *Attention Deficit Hyperactivity Disorder.* Washington, DC: Author.

Patel, H. (1996). Lecture on AD/HD at Highland Park Learning Center, Roanoke, VA.

Stevens, L. J., Zentall, S. S., Deck, J. L., Abate, M. L., Watkins, B. A., Lipp, S. R., & Burgess, J. R. (1995). Essential fatty acid metabolism in boys with Attention-Deficit/Hyperactivity Disorder. *American Journal of Clinical Nutrition, 62,* 761–768.

Sylwester, R. (1995). *A celebration of neurons: An educator's guide to the human brain.* Alexandria, VA: Association for Supervision and Curriculum Development.

Turecki, S. (1997, November). *Practical psychopharmacology for children.* Paper presented at the meeting of the Nurse Practitioner Associates for Continuing Education (NPACE), Boston, MA.

Viadero, D. (1996, September 18). Brain trust. *Education Week, 16*(3), 31–33.

Weiss, G. (1990). Hyperactivity in childhood. *The New England Journal of Medicine, 323*(20), 1413–1415.

Studies on the Cause(s) of Attention Deficit/Hyperactivity Disorder

The clearest way into the universe is through a forest.

—John Muir

In order to understand Attention Deficit/Hyperactivity Disorder (AD/HD), it is essential that one understands the underlying causes. When we form opinions based on observations alone, we may jump to erroneous conclusions. Because AD/HD is primarily recognizable by behavioral manifestations, it is easy to see why some people assume that these behaviors are learned and controllable. Such behaviors are often blamed on poor parenting or a lack of discipline. The assumption is sometimes made that if a child can sit still to watch a favorite television show, then it is within the child's ability to control the behavior in other situations. By reviewing the evidence of a neurological origin of AD/HD, readers can reexamine their own beliefs on the nature of the disorder and be able to speak about and approach the subject from a more informed and mindful position.

For a period of time it was theorized that excessive motor activity and impulsivity were caused by diet. One of the more well-known treatments along these lines is the Feingold Diet, which, although successful with a small percentage of children, has not been supported by research findings (Gross, Tofanelli, Butzirus, & Snodgrass, 1987; Mattes & Gittelman, 1981).

Even though the misconception persists that AD/HD is the result of permissive parenting or junk food diets, numerous studies have been done that indicate a neurological basis for the disorder. However, socio-cultural factors such as parenting and diet may contribute to the expression of AD/HD and associated disorders.

AD/HD is not a new phenomenon. Although the labels and theories may have changed over time, AD/HD has long been recognized as a dysfunctional condition occurring in some children. As far back as 1890, William James proposed that the characteristics we now associate with AD/HD in children had a neurological basis. At the beginning of the 20th century research began on this complex disorder and has continued and increased tremendously in recent years (Barkley, 1990).

Due to the complex nature of AD/HD, it has been difficult for researchers to identify a specific cause or causes for the disorder. Therefore, in spite of the extensive studies that have been conducted, there is no known cause; but there are a number of theories with some modest or isolated support. The following reviews are a sample of current research studies and findings regarding genetic and environmental causes and the debate over nature versus nurture. There are also studies cited that indicate that there may be specific physical differences, particularly in the brain, between individuals with and without AD/HD.

GENETIC FACTORS

1. **Evidence of Familial Association between Attention Deficit Disorder and Major Affective Disorders.** Joseph Biederman, Stephen Faraone, Kate Keenan, and Ming Tsuang. (1991). *Archives of General Psychiatry, 48,* 633–642.

The subjects in this study were white males between the ages of 6 and 17 years. There were 73 individuals with Attention Deficit Disorder (ADD) and 264 of their relatives; 26 without ADD and 92 of their relatives. Of the subjects with ADD, 33% also met the criteria for Affective Disorders (AFF), which included depression, Bipolar Disorder, and Mood Disorder. All subjects had an I.Q. of at least 70. The purpose was to see if there was a relationship between the occurrence of ADD and major AFF within families to determine a genetic link.

Two environmental factors were considered for possible relevance (social class and intactness of family), and neither was found to be associated with an increased risk of AFF in subjects with ADD or their relatives. It appears that ADD and AFF may have a common etiological basis, which means that whatever causes one may also cause the other. The findings from this study are based on clinically referred subjects that are typically more severely ill than nonreferred subjects; therefore, the results cannot be generalized to the population at large.

It was found that relatives of children with ADD and AFF were at a greater risk of having either of those disorders than relatives of normal individuals. The implications are there for the need to develop early intervention programs for youth at risk of having ADD and AFF. The authors suggest that further research needs to be done to determine the nature of the familial relationship between ADD and AFF, as well as any environmental factors that may come into play.

2. **Further Evidence for Family-Genetic Risk Factors in Attention Deficit Hyperactivity Disorder.** Joseph Biederman, Stephen Faraone, Kate Keenan, Jonathan Benjamin, Belinda Krifcher, Cindy Moore, Susan Sprich-Buckminster, Karen Ugaglia, Michael Jellinek, Ronald Steingard, Thomas Spencer, Dennis Norman, Roselyn Kolodny, Ilana Kraus, James Perrin, Martin Keller, and Ming Tsuang. (1992). *Archives of General Psychiatry, 49,* 47–57.

Joseph Biederman and colleagues have been involved in extensive research on AD/HD, particularly its occurrence within families and the co-occurrence of AD/HD with other disorders, such as Conduct Disorder (CD), Mood and Anxiety Disorder, and Antisocial Disorder. Along with an increased risk of AD/HD among relatives, there also appears to be an increased risk for one of the associated disorders along with AD/HD. In spite of the fact that most of the research has focused on male subjects, there is some evidence that indicates that relatives of females with AD/HD are also at a higher risk of AD/HD, as well as anxiety, antisocial, and depressive disorders, than relatives of non-AD/HD individuals. Due to the co-occurrence of other disorders with AD/HD, studying the disorder is complicated by the variety of combinations that may occur.

In this study the researchers explored the relationship between the occurrence of AD/HD within families and that of other psychiatric disorders to determine if distinct subgroups exist. They also considered whether or not AD/HD is associated with a genetic vulnerability for associated disorders. In other words, they evaluated the increased risk for anxiety disorders, CD, and Mood Disorder in individuals with AD/HD. The study involved 140 children with AD/HD, 120 normal children, and their 822 first-degree relatives (parents, brothers, and sisters). Data were gathered through the use of structured interviews with parents, siblings, and subjects, except children under 12 years of age. Socioeconomic status (SES) was controlled by excluding the lowest category (SES-VI). Subjects with major sensorimotor handicaps, psychosis, autism, or I.Q. scores below 80 were also excluded.

Although SES and family intactness are recognized as influential factors, they did not account for the risk of AD/HD and other disorders within families, except in two instances. After controlling for SES, both the risk for CD (see Appendix C for APA definition) and substance dependency could not be explained by family-genetic factors. The interaction between genes and environment is a factor that cannot be overlooked. One's place within the family, peer relationships, and parental separation or divorce and the resulting impact on income and residence are all environmental family factors that may increase the risk of CD and substance dependency in children with AD/HD. It is also possible that CD with AD/HD may be a distinct subtype of AD/HD.

In conclusion, Biederman and colleagues believe that their findings in this study lend further support to previous findings of a genetic cause of AD/HD and selected associated disorders. They also recognize the complexity of the disorder and suggest that AD/HD is "a group of conditions" rather than one distinct disorder. Therefore, a number of causes may exist. Continued research is necessary to validate the subtypes, and their causes, including a closer look at environmental factors.

3. **Genetic Heterogeneity in Attention-Deficit Hyperactivity Disorder (AD/HD): Gender, Psychiatric Comorbidity, and Maternal AD/HD.** Stephen Faraone, Joseph Biederman, Wei Chen, Sharon Milberger, Rebecca Warburton, and Ming Tsuang. (1995). *Journal of Abnormal Psychology, 104*(2), 334–345.

Definition of Terms

comorbidity: co-ocurrence with other conditions (Castellanos, 1997a)

heterogeneity: a quality or state of being heterogeneous (*Merriam-Webster's*, 1987, p.568)

heterogeneous: consisting of dissimilar or diverse ingredients or constituents: MIXED (*Merriam-Webster's*, 1987, p.568)

Teachers are familiar with heterogeneous reading groups in which there is a mixture of students with diverse or varying reading ability levels. In the context of this article, heterogeneity refers to the variation of characteristics and combinations of conditions occurring with AD/HD. As one would imagine, the more complex the disorder, the more difficult it is to study it. This is the case with AD/HD, and it seems that the more we study it the more complexities we discover.

The authors of this study attempted to unravel some of the confounding aspects of AD/HD by studying how gender and the presence of antisocial disorders might affect siblings of boys with the disorder. Families were considered antisocial if either the subject or a parent had Antisocial Personality Disorder, which is characterized by "a pattern of covert antisocial acts such as fire setting, truancy, stealing, and vandalism" (Barkley, 1990, p.165). "The diagnosis of Antisocial Personality Disorder cannot be given to individuals under age 18 years" (APA, 1994, p.90).

Stephen Faraone and colleagues found that boys from antisocial families with mothers diagnosed with AD/HD are at the greatest risk for AD/HD. The risk for AD/HD is the same for brothers and sisters from families that are not antisocial. There may be a distinct genetic subtype of AD/HD with CD (see Appendix C for APA definition) that occurs in antisocial families, whereas, individuals with AD/HD from non-antisocial families are at a greater risk for depression and Oppositional Defiant Disorder (ODD) (see Appendix D for APA definition).

4. **Attention-Deficit Hyperactivity Disorder in People with Generalized Resistance to Thyroid Hormone.** Peter Hauser, Alan Zametkin, Pedro Martinez, Benedetto Vitiello, John Matochik, A. James Mixson, and Bruce Weintraub. (1993). *The New England Journal of Medicine, 328*(14), 997–1000.

Symptoms of AD/HD are often seen in individuals with generalized resistance to thyroid hormone. This is a disease in which a mutation in a thyroid gene renders tissues less receptive to thyroid hormone. Eighteen families with a history of generalized resistance to thyroid hormone were included in the study. Within these families, 49 members were affected with generalized resistance to thyroid hormone, and 55 were unaffected. There were 52 adults and 52 children. Structured interviews were conducted to determine if the subjects met the criteria for AD/HD.

The adults with the thyroid disorder were 15 times more likely to have AD/HD; children with the thyroid disorder were 10 times more likely to have AD/HD. All of the subjects in the study had similar genetic and environmental backgrounds, except for the receptor gene mutation in the family members affected with generalized resistance to thyroid hormone. In addition, the researchers found that the risk for AD/HD for males in both groups (affected and unaffected with thyroid disorder) was three times as great as that of the females. This lends support to the general belief that AD/HD is more prevalent among males than females.

The thyroid receptor gene may play a role in brain development, particularly during critical prenatal stages. It may also influence the development and interaction between neurotransmitters involved in AD/HD in the human brain. A neurotransmitter is a chemical in the brain that relays messages. One implication of the findings in this study is that less overt thyroid dysfunction may be underlying AD/HD in cases that otherwise seem unrelated, such as low secretion of thyroid hormone. Another implication is for the use of thyroid hormone in the treatment of AD/HD in the appropriate situations. *It is important to keep in mind that this research looks at the chemical interactions in the brain in relation to the mutated thyroid gene as a cause of AD/HD behaviors, not the behaviors related to a lowered secretion of thyroid hormone, which might be quite different.*

Letters to the Editor

5. **Learning Disorders and the Thyroid.** Vinod Bhatara, J. Michael McMillin, Raymond Tervo, and Francis Bandettini. (1996). *Journal of American Academy of Child and Adolescent Psychiatry, 35*(4), 406–407.

In a letter to the editor, Vinod Bhatara and colleagues emphasize the point that since thyroid dysfunction is associated with cognitive functioning, teachers may be the first ones to witness the onset of academic difficulties. For this reason, they contend, teachers must be aware of the importance of a medical referral in such cases.

6. **Etiology of AD/HD: Nature or Nurture?** Lawrence Diller, J. Lane Tanner, and Jon Weil. (1996). *American Journal of Psychiatry, 153*(3), 451–452.

Even among researchers there is some debate over whether AD/HD is caused by genetics or environment. Joseph Biederman and Stephen Faraone have conducted numerous studies on AD/HD, several of which are cited above. Although the focus of their research has primarily been on genetic causes for the disorder, they have also done some studies on environmental factors, as cited below.

In the Letters to the Editors column of the *American Journal of Psychiatry*, Lawrence Diller, J. Lane Tanner, and Jon Weil criticize Biederman and Faraone for overemphasizing genetics at the expense of environment as causal factors, and for the resulting implication that medication is therefore the only treatment. They also point out some perceived flaws in the research design that uses telephone interviews, which in their opinion contributes to the overdiagnoses of AD/HD.

Reply. Joseph Biederman and Stephen Faraone. (1996). *American Journal of Psychiatry, 153*(3), 452.

Within the same issue of the journal, Biederman and Faraone responded to the comments made by Diller, Tanner, and Weil by criticizing their limited thinking. In their rebuttal, Beiderman and Faraone clarify their findings regarding environment versus genetics and recognize the need for more research on environmental factors.

As we review the research, it is important to keep in mind the fact that even the researchers are debating and grappling for answers regarding the cause or causes of AD/HD.

ENVIRONMENTAL FACTORS

7. **Is Maternal Smoking during Pregnancy a Risk Factor for Attention Deficit/Hyperactivity Disorder in Children?** Sharon Milberger, Joseph Biederman, Stephen Faraone, Lisa Chen, and Janice Jones. (1996). *American Journal of Psychiatry, 153*(9), 1138–1142.

Sharon Milberger and colleagues compared 140 boys between the ages of 6 and 17 who were diagnosed with AD/HD with 120 normal boys of the same age, and the first-degree biological relatives of both groups of subjects. A standardized rating system was used to gather information on the mother's smoking habits during pregnancy. It was found that in the group being studied only 8% of normal subjects had mothers who smoked during pregnancy while 22% of the AD/HD children were exposed to maternal smoking during pregnancy. The results also indicated significant I.Q. differences between the children of mothers who smoked during pregnancy and those who did not (with an average I.Q. score of almost 11 points lower for the children of smoking mothers).

Animal studies using pregnant mice and rats support the association between chronic exposure to nicotine and increased activity in the young. In the study of children, chronic exposure was defined as being at least three months in duration.

The authors were concerned about other variables affecting the results, such as parents' I.Q.s, parental AD/HD, and the SES of the family. Compared to the normal control group, AD/HD subjects were from families with a slightly lower SES and had a higher incidence of mothers and fathers with AD/HD and with lower I.Q.s. However, when these factors were taken into account, there was still a significant association between maternal smoking and AD/HD.

Low-birth-weight (LBW), which has been associated with maternal smoking during pregnancy, was not considered to be an influencing factor in this study as none of the children exposed to maternal smoking were of LBW or under five pounds at birth. Ruling out this factor lends further support to the findings associating maternal smoking with lower cognitive function and AD/HD.

Limitations of this study include the difficulty involved in obtaining accurate and unbiased reflective accounts from the mothers of their smoking habits during pregnancy; the authors did not account for prenatal exposure to secondhand smoke; and the subjects with AD/HD had been selected on the basis of their clinical referral; therefore, the results cannot be generalized to the general population.

In conclusion, the authors indicated a possible AD/HD risk associated with maternal smoking with implications for additional research to confirm these findings as well as programs focusing on smoking prevention or cessation for mothers during pregnancy.

8. **Psychiatric Sequelae of Low-birth-weight at 6 Years of Age.** Naomi
   Breslau, Gregory Brown, Jerel DelDotto, Savitri Kumar, Sudhakar Ezhuthachan, Patricia Andreski, and Karen Hufnagle. (1996). *Journal of Abnormal Child Psychology*, 24(3), 385–400.

Definition of Term

sequelae: an aftereffect of disease or injury (*Merriam-Webster's*, 1987, p.1073)

The purpose of this study was to examine the relationship between LBW and AD/HD. The subjects, 473 LBW and 350 normal-birth-weight (NBW) children, were randomly selected from both urban and suburban hospital records. Through the use of parent and child interviews, behavior rating scales by teachers, and a thorough neuropsychological evaluation of the children, the subjects were diagnosed for Anxiety Disorder (characterized by excessive worry and anxiety [APA, 1994]), ODD (see Appendix D for APA definition), overanxiousness, and AD/HD. Both mothers and children were evaluated for I.Q.

The results suggested an association between LBW and AD/HD, but not the other childhood disorders such as Anxiety Disorder and ODD, and the association was stronger in urban populations than in suburban populations. The authors excluded children with severe disabilities. There was a higher rate of AD/HD among LBW subjects with lower I.Q. scores than subjects with average or above I.Q. scores. With I.Q. levels at or above 100, the likelihood of an AD/HD diagnosis was the same for LBW as NBW children.

The authors noted the beneficial effects a suburban environment might have on a child, thus mitigating the risks of AD/HD in that group of children. In addition, mothers in suburban settings may have underreported the symptoms of AD/HD, but this should have been corrected for by the teacher rating scales. Due to the fact that data on family histories were not available, there may be other unidentified factors that predispose a child to AD/HD, and LBW increases the risk. Further research is needed to address family vulnerability and AD/HD.

PHYSIOLOGICAL BRAIN DIFFERENCES

In this section, brain differences are addressed in support of a physiological basis for AD/HD, but no attempt is made to establish a causal relationship between these differences and AD/HD. Such a relationship has not been established through research findings. The reader needs to keep this in mind when reading this section and not assume that the authors are implying a causal relationship.

9. **Psychiatric Outcomes in Low-birth-weight Children at Age 6 Years: Relation to Neonatal Cranial Ultrasound Abnormalities.** Agnes Whitaker, Ronan Van Rossem, Judith Feldman, Sam Schonfeld, Jennifer Pinto-Martin, Carolyn Torre, David Shaffer, and Nigel Paneth. (1997). *Archives of General Psychiatry, 54,* 847–856.

Definition of Terms

psychiatric disorders (outcomes): in this study they include, but are not limited to, Attention Deficit/Hyperactivity Disorder, Tic Disorders, Oppositional Defiant Disorder, Obsessive-Compulsive Disorder, and nocturnal enuresis (bed-wetting) (Whitaker et al., 1997)

sequelae: an aftereffect of disease or injury (*Merriam-Webster's*, 1987, p.1073)

ultrasonography: a diagnostic technique for the examination of internal body structures (*Merriam-Webster's*, 1987, p.1280)

ultrasound: vibrations of the same physical nature as sound but with frequencies above the range of human hearing (*Merriam-Webster's*, 1987, p.1280)

Through the use of ultrasonography it is now possible to study LBW newborns for brain damage and the effects on later behavioral manifestations or psychiatric outcomes. The purpose of this study was to see if there were detectable brain differences in children who were later identified as having some type of psychiatric disorder, including AD/HD. The subjects were a group of LBW babies born over a 2.5 year period. An ultrasonography was done within a week of birth to determine if there were any brain abnormalities. A follow-up evaluation was done on the same group of children at six years of age to determine if they had any of the psychiatric outcomes previously mentioned.

The results showed that 80% of the children in the sample had normal ultrasonography readings, indicating that no brain abnormalities were detected. For the remaining children, differences were found in specific locations in the brain. Within the entire sample, 22% had at least one psychiatric disorder, with most having more than one disorder. AD/HD was the most frequently occurring disorder. Boys had a much higher incidence than girls for any of the disorders.

The researchers looked at indicators of psychiatric disorder other than brain abnormalities identified by ultrasound. They found that the risk of psychiatric outcome was increased by maternal smoking, male sex, and social disadvantage in the child's immediate environment. *These factors have been identified and supported by previously reviewed studies within this chapter.*

In conclusion, the findings of this study suggest a relationship between specific types of damage to the brain that may accompany LBW and the occurrence of AD/HD, and it appears that the risk may be increased by gender, maternal smoking, and social disadvantage in the immediate environment.

10. **Association of Attention-Deficit Disorder and the Dopamine Transporter Gene.** Edwin H. Cook, Mark Stein, Matthew Krasowski, Nancy Cox, Deborah Olkon, John Kieffer, and Bennett Leventhal. (1995). *American Journal of Human Genetics 56, 993–998.*

Definition of Terms

dopamine: neurotransmitter; brain messenger (Castellanos, 1997a, p.34)

dopamine transporter: a chemical which facilitates the reabsorption of dopamine (Castellanos, 1997a)

gene: a carrier of heredity (Lefrancois, 1996, p.565)

neuron: a nerve cell (Castellanos, 1997a, p.31)

neurotransmitter: a substance that transmits nerve impulses across a synapse (*Merriam-Webster's*, 1987, p.795)

synapse: the point at which a nervous impulse passes from one neuron to another (*Merriam-Webster's*, 1987, p.1196)

Dopamine, a chemical in the brain that relays messages, has been implicated as an area of possible dysfunction in AD/HD. Typically, dopamine is broken down quickly after it is released in the body. If for some reason the breakdown and reabsorption is delayed, it is theorized that high levels of hyperactivity, inattention, and impulsivity result. Due to the success of medications that regulate the reabsorption of dopamine in patients with AD/HD, the authors of this study were interested in the part dopamine plays in the disorder. Coming from the perspective that AD/HD is familial, they designed their study with a focus on families with AD/HD and administered intelligence tests, behavior rating scales, and DNA testing. The family units consisted of the mother, father, and the affected child or children.

Edwin Cook and colleagues concluded that, although these results need to be replicated to determine if there are any defective gene patterns, there appears to be some association between mutations in the dopamine transporter gene and the manifestation of AD/HD within families. This is an indication of a difference in brain chemistry among individuals with AD/HD and those without the disorder, and it reinforces the theory of heritability.

11. **Essential Fatty Acid Metabolism in Boys with Attention-Deficit/Hyperactivity Disorder.** Laura J. Stevens, Sydney S. Zentall, John L. Deck, Marcey L. Abate, Bruce A. Watkins, Steven R. Lipp, and John R. Burgess. (1995). *American Journal of Clinical Nutrition, 62,* 761–768.

The purpose of this study was to determine if essential fatty acid (EFA) is associated with AD/HD in boys. EFA plays an important part in the structure and function of the cells in the human body. Subjects included in the study consisted of boys with AD/HD and a control group of healthy boys (all between the ages of 6 and 12 years). The AD/HD diagnosis was confirmed through parent and teacher completion of behavior rating scales. EFA levels were determined by blood tests.

Results

AD/HD subjects had lower levels of EFA than controls. In addition, they had some of the symptoms of EFA deficiency, such as thirst (greater fluid intake), more frequent urination, and drier skin than the control group. *If there is a subtype of AD/HD associated with EFA deficiency, these students may be genuinely thirsty and need to use the restroom more often than other students, rather than just displaying these behaviors as an excuse to leave the room. It has been my experience that some students with AD/HD more frequently requested drinks of water and restroom "passes." I typically attributed this behavior to their short attention spans and restless energy, but this study points out some other factors that we as teachers need to be cognizant of in meeting the individual needs of our students.*

12. **Relationships between Serum Free Fatty Acids and Zinc, and Attention Deficit Hyperactivity Disorder: A Research Note.** Mehmet Bekaroglu, Yakup Aslan, Yusuf Gedik, Orhan Deger, Hilal Mocan, Erol Erduran, and Caner Karahan. (1996). *Journal of Child Psychology and Psychiatry, 37*(2), 225–227.

Some studies have indicated a possible association between deficiencies in zinc and EFA and hyperactivity or maladjusted behavior. There has also been a great deal in the press in recent years about serotonin and melatonin and their effects on mood and behavior. In a quest for answers about how the brain functions, scientists have been studying the actions and interactions of chemicals in the brain. For example, zinc and fatty acids are believed to influence the production of serotonin and melatonin, which in turn affect dopamine function. So it seems reasonable to study deficiencies in zinc and EFA in relationship to AD/HD.

Other studies have linked both zinc and EFA, individually, to hyperactivity (see Study #11). These authors looked at the levels of both elements in patients with AD/HD. The research was conducted by establishing a diagnosis of AD/HD for the target group and by analyzing free fatty acid (FFA) and zinc levels from blood samples. The subjects included boys and girls between the ages of 6 1/2 and 12 years.

The authors' hypothesis was confirmed by findings that children with AD/HD had significantly lower levels of zinc and FFA than the control group. It is not clear whether the zinc deficiency is responsible for the lowered FFA levels; further studies are needed to establish FFA as a primary or perhaps secondary cause of AD/HD.

As educators we should be aware of reports of poor response to stimulant treatment (i.e., Ritalin and Cylert) on the part of AD/HD children diagnosed with zinc deficiencies (Bekaroglu et al., 1996). This is another example of the heterogeneous nature of AD/HD and why some students do not seem to respond to the typical medications prescribed for the disorder. The implications are clear for the need, on the part of teachers, to not only have a better understanding of the biological basis of AD/HD, but also to take a team approach, working collaboratively with parents and physicians in dealing with treatment and interventions.

MAGNETIC RESONANCE IMAGING AND PHYSIOLOGICAL BRAIN DIFFERENCES

The following three studies involve the use of magnetic resonance imaging (MRI) as a research tool. Magnetic resonance imaging is a nonintrusive method of studying anatomy or, in these three cases, the human brain by obtaining high resolution images. This technique does not expose the subject to dangerous radiation and therefore can be used safely with children. Specific sites in the brain have been implicated in AD/HD, and through the use of MRI, abnormalities at these sites can be identified (Ernst, 1996).

13. **Quantitative Morphology of the Caudate Nucleus in Attention Deficit Hyperactivity Disorder.** F. Xavier Castellanos, Jay N. Giedd, Paul Eckburg, Wendy L. Marsh, A. Catherine Vaituzis, Debra Kaysen, Susan D. Hamburger, and Judith L. Rapoport. (1994). *American Journal of Psychiatry, 151*(12), 1791–1796.

Executive functions have been defined as "control processes . . . [involving] inhibition and delay of responding [allowing an individual to] initiate, sustain, inhibit/stop and shift." Also associated with the construct of executive function are the abilities to prioritize, organize, and strategize. (Castellanos, 1997b, p.4)

Any teacher who has worked with a student with AD/HD has witnessed a deficit in one or more of the areas identified as executive functions. Such students typically have difficulty shifting from one activity to another, controlling impulsive behaviors (most commonly seen as calling out answers), and commanding organizational skills. These very behaviors are what educators find most challenging in the classroom. F. Xavier Castellanos and colleagues conducted a comparison of male subjects with AD/HD and those without, looking for differences in brain structure and size in the areas of the brain associated with executive function. The methods used consisted of MRI scans to measure brain volume and symmetry of all the subjects. They hypothesized that there would be differences between the two groups corresponding to deficits in executive function in the AD/HD group.

Asymmetry (a difference in measurement or proportion between two sides) is normal in the human brain. It has been found in this and other studies that the degree of asymmetry for boys with AD/HD is less than that of the "normal" control group of non-AD/HD boys. In addition, these authors report a smaller brain volume in subjects with the disorder. These differences in symmetry and size may account for the manifestation of behaviors associated with deficits in executive function.

It is essential that teachers understand that anatomical differences may be associated with the behaviors exhibited by students with AD/HD. If the condition has a physiological basis, it may not be within the student's power to control undesirable behaviors. More research is necessary in this area, especially through studies that include female subjects. The issue of gender, which will be discussed later in this chapter, is identified as an area for future study by these authors.

14. **Quantitative Brain Magnetic Resonance Imaging in Attention Deficit/Hyperactivity Disorder.** F. Xavier Castellanos, Jay N. Giedd, Wendy L. Marsh, Susan D. Hamburger, A. Catherine Vaituzis, Daniel P. Dickstein, Stacy Sarfatti, Yolanda Vauss, John Snell, Nicholas Lange, Debra Kaysen, Amy L. Krain, Gail F. Ritchie, Jagath C. Rajapakse, and Judith L. Rapoport. (1996). *Archives of General Psychiatry, 53,* 607–616.

The previous study by the same leading authors, published in 1994 (see Study #13), focused primarily on the caudate nucleus. In an attempt to measure a wider range of brain regions, Castellanos et al. (Study #14) used MRI to determine if there were structural differences associated with AD/HD.

The results of both studies were similar in that the subjects with AD/HD had smaller overall brain size and differences in asymmetry when compared with non-AD/HD controls. The authors feel the results of this research lend support to a physiological basis for AD/HD based on structural brain differences. The subject group consisted of males only and the findings cannot be generalized to females.

GENDER DIFFERENCES

Although gender is not actually a causal factor in AD/HD, it is included in this chapter as a biological/physiological difference. There may be variations in the manifestation of AD/HD between males and females, which could influence the selection of interventions. An awareness of the differences or similarities between males and females with AD/HD may be beneficial to educators in evaluating which intervention to implement for a specific student.

The relationship between gender differences and AD/HD has been identified as an area needing more research. There are not many studies available for review. In the study that was selected, the authors reviewed 18 other studies on gender and AD/HD. By using this method of review, the authors are able to present an overview of the findings. It is also an indication of the limited amount of research that has been done.

15. **Gender Differences in AD/HD: A Meta-Analysis and Critical Review.** Miranda Gaub and Caryn L. Carlson. (1997). *Journal of American Academy of Child and Adolescent Psychiatry, 36*(8), 1036–1045.

The overwhelming majority of research on AD/HD has been conducted on male subjects. The reason for this is that the disorder has been observed to occur more frequently in males, and it is also a way to limit the number of variables in each study (Ernst, 1996). However, the research findings may be different for females, and if girls are not included in the studies, then the findings cannot be generalized to include them.

Miranda Gaub and Caryn L. Carlson conducted a meta-analysis of research on gender differences in AD/HD. A meta-analysis is an analysis of a number of studies that focus on the same question and use similar variables (Ary, Jacobs, & Razavieh, 1996). Due to the limited amount of research that has been done on gender and AD/HD, the authors had difficulty finding appropriate studies. They were able to find 18 studies that met their criteria for size and selected variables. Therefore, by reviewing this meta-analysis we are able to review the cumulative results of a group of studies rather than just one isolated study.

The results have significant implications for educators. There are distinct differences between girls with AD/HD who have been clinically referred and girls with AD/HD who have not been clinically referred when compared to boys with AD/HD. The following chart outlines the results of the meta-analysis.

Clinically Referred Girls with AD/HD

Girls (compared to boys):

- lower levels of hyperactivity
- fewer diagnosed with conduct disorders
- lower rate of externalizing behavior (acting out behaviors)
- greater intellectual impairment
- greater severity of inattention

Similar levels of:

- internalizing behavior
- aggression toward peers
- disliking peers

Nonreferred Girls with AD/HD

Show less impairment than boys on:

- inattention
- internalizing behaviors
- aggression toward peers
- disliking peers

Both boys and girls with AD/HD were characteristically of a lower SES than non-AD/HD children, but girls with AD/HD were of a lower SES than boys with AD/HD, or, in other words, they were found to be at a greater social disadvantage.

The results of this analysis suggest that girls with AD/HD are more likely to have learning problems while boys with AD/HD are more likely to exhibit behavior problems. Within a structured learning environment, behavior problems probably lead to more referrals, whereas learning problems are probably addressed within the context of the school setting. This may partially account for a lower referral rate of girls for clinic-based treatment. *Since AD/HD may present itself differently in girls and boys, how we respond to our students will no doubt vary also.*

The authors identified some limitations in their study, including the small number of studies available addressing gender differences and AD/HD. There was also the constraint of having primarily clinically referred populations from which to draw results. Since girls are less likely to be referred to a clinic, those females included in the research are probably more severe, atypical cases. The differences between clinically referred boys and girls were minimal, but the girls in this category are not necessarily representative of the majority of girls with AD/HD; therefore, the results are not widely generalizable.

Gaub and Carlson feel that the results of their meta-analysis should be used with caution and strongly recommend that more research be done addressing the nature of AD/HD in girls. *This caution is particularly pertinent to educators who must keep gender differences in mind when working with AD/HD students. We cannot generalize the research findings with disregard for gender and severity, but must be mindful and observant of individual differences among our students.*

CHAPTER SUMMARY

The 15 studies reviewed in this chapter are representative of the research that is being done in the areas identified as causal or differences associated with AD/HD. This is by no means considered a comprehensive coverage of the research. However, through this review we as educators should be better prepared to speak knowledgeably to others on the subject. In addition, we should be able to develop our own beliefs on the nature of the disorder. Although the review may not be comprehensive, there is nevertheless an abundance of information to synthesize. In an effort to provide an easy-to-read format, I have summarized the purpose, results, and implications of the studies in Table 2.1. Educators can, at a glance, see what each study indicates in relation to meaningful interactions with individuals with AD/HD and their families.

As illustrated in the table: (1) four studies address genetic factors, (2) two articles deal with environmental factors, (3) physiological differences are reviewed in six studies, and (4) only male subjects were used in seven cases and both genders were represented in four studies. Although the research has been categorized into specific areas for organizational purposes, there is a great deal of overlap among the research in each of the areas. It is difficult to study genetics without considering environmental influences or physiological differences without taking genetic factors into account. Thus, we are only beginning to see the complexity of the disorder, and much more research is needed to truly understand what causes AD/HD. At least as educators we can begin to put the research in perspective and recognize the importance of keeping informed on current findings to enhance our effectiveness in the classroom and with parents and other professionals.

Table 2.1
Summary of Results of Studies on Causes

Topic/Purpose	Interpretations	Implications
Genetic Factors		
1. Genetic link between AD/HD and Affective Disorder	Found a relationship between occurrence of AD/HD and Affective Disorder within families	Need for early identification and intervention to improve outcome
Male subjects only		
2. Familial-genetic cause for AD/HD and associated disorders	• Hypothesis supported complexity of disorder • Environmental factors • Conduct Disorder with AD/HD may be a subtype	• Further support of a genetic basis • Need to consider environment's impact on AD/HD students
Male subjects only		
3. Gender, comorbidity, and maternal AD/HD as factors in AD/HD	• Reinforces Conduct Disorder with AD/HD as subtype • Considers environmental and family factors	Heterogeneity of disorder means confounding factors and need to consider individual differences
Male subjects only		
4. Relationship between generalized resistance to thyroid hormone and AD/HD	• Results indicate adults with thyroid disorder are 15 times more likely to have AD/HD; children 10 times more likely • Use of thyroid hormone suggested for AD/HD when indicated	• Reinforces physiological basis for AD/HD • Suggests another treatment in cases of generalized resistance to thyroid hormone for doctors to consider
Male and female subjects		
5. Letter to editor	Emphasizes role of educator in identification	• Teachers may be the first to observe academic difficulties that are due to thyroid dysfunction • Awareness of need for medical referral
6. Letters to editor: Nature versus nurture in AD/HD etiology	• Need for more research on genetics and environment • Debate among researchers	Educators should be aware of possible multiple causes of AD/HD; researchers still unsure

Table 2.1 (*continued*)

Topic/Purpose	Interpretations	Implications
Environmental Factors		
7. Maternal smoking during pregnancy as a risk factor in AD/HD Male subjects only	• Lower amount (8%) of maternal smoking during pregnancy for normal subjects • Higher amount (22%) for AD/HD group, and lower I.Q. scores	Educational efforts at smoking prevention and cessation for mothers during pregnancy
8. Examines relationship between low-birth-weight and AD/HD Male and female subjects	• Suggests association between low-birth-weight and AD/HD • Stronger association in urban than suburban populations	Teacher awareness of risk factors may lead to early identification and intervention
Physiological Brain Differences		
9. Relationship between low-birth-weight ultrasound abnormalities and AD/HD Male and female subjects	• Associates AD/HD with low-birth-weight and ultrasound abnormalities • Additional risk factors include maternal smoking, male sex, social disadvantage	• Awareness of association between brain and AD/HD • Awareness of risk factors
10. Genetic influence on dopamine and AD/HD	• Supports genetic basis for AD/HD • Neurotransmitter activity impacts upon AD/HD manifestation	Awareness of familial factors in AD/HD
11. Association between essential fatty acid levels and AD/HD Male subjects only	• AD/HD subjects had lower essential fatty acid levels • AD/HD subjects had some symptoms of essential fatty acid deficiency: thirst, frequent urination, with dry skin	• Sensitivity to need for more frequent drinks of water and use of restrooms • Awareness of signs of essential fatty acid deficiency with AD/HD for possible medical referral

Table 2.1 (*continued*)

Topic/Purpose	Interpretations	Implications
12. Deficiencies in zinc and essential fatty acid associated with AD/HD Male and female subjects	Lower levels of zinc and essential fatty acid in AD/HD group	Children with zinc deficiencies typically do not respond to amphetamine treatment for AD/HD. If a student is not responding to medication (Ritalin/Cylert) it may be due to a zinc deficiency and the teacher should communicate this to the child's physician.

Magnetic Resonance Imaging Studies

Topic/Purpose	Interpretations	Implications
13. Executive function and brain abnormalities Male subjects only	Less than normal asymmetry and brain volume in AD/HD subjects	Awareness of role executive function plays in classroom performance (impulsivity, organization, and study skills)
14. Brain differences associated with AD/HD Male subjects only	Subjects with AD/HD had smaller brain size and differences in asymmetry	Awareness of a physiological basis for AD/HD; enhanced communication with parents

Gender Differences

Topic/Purpose	Interpretations	Implications
15. Meta-analysis of gender and AD/HD	• Limited number of studies • Girls showed greater intellectual impairment • Boys greater behavioral problems	• Teachers should be aware of gender differences in AD/HD • Do not overgeneralize these findings as more research is needed

REFERENCES

American Psychiatric Association (APA). (1994). *Diagnostic and statistical manual of mental disorders* (4th ed.). Washington, DC: Author.

Ary, D., Jacobs, L., & Razavieh, A. (1996). *Introduction to research in education.* Orlando: Holt, Rinehart, & Winston.

Barkley, R. A. (1990). *Attention Deficit Hyperactivity Disorder: A handbook for diagnosis and treatment.* New York: Guilford Press.

Bekaroglu, M., Aslan, Y., Gedik, Y., Deger, O., Mocan, H., Erduran, E., & Karahan, C. (1996). Relationships between serum free fatty acids and zinc, and Attention Deficit Hyperactivity Disorder: A research note. *Journal of Child Psychology and Psychiatry, 37*(2), 225–227.

Bhatara, V., McMillin, J. M., Tervo, R., & Bandettini, F. (1996). Learning disorders and the thyroid [Letter to the editor]. *Journal of American Academy of Child and Adolescent Psychiatry, 35*(4), 406–407.

Biederman, J., & Faraone, S. (1996). Reply [Letter to the editor]. *American Journal of Psychiatry, 153*(3), 452.

Biederman, J., Faraone, S., Keenan, K., Benjamin, J., Krifcher, B., Moore, C., Sprich-Buckminster, S., Ugaglia, K., Jellinek, M., Steingard, R., Spencer, T., Norman, D., Kolodny, R., Kraus, I., Perrin, J., Keller, M., & Tsuang, M. (1992, September). Further evidence for family-genetic risk factors in Attention Deficit Hyperactivity Disorder. *Archives of General Psychiatry, 49*, 47–57.

Biederman, J., Faraone, S., Keenan, K., & Tsuang, M. (1991). Evidence of familial association between Attention Deficit Disorder and Major Affective Disorders. *Archives of General Psychiatry, 48*, 633–642.

Breslau, N., Brown, G., DelDotto, J., Kumar, S., Ezhuthachan, S., Andreski, P., & Hufnagle, K. (1996). Psychiatric sequelae of low-birth-weight at 6 years of age. *Journal of Abnormal Child Psychology, 24*(3), 385–400.

Castellanos, F. X. (1997a). Approaching a scientific understanding of what happens in the brain in AD/HD. *Attention, 4*(1), 30–35.

Castellanos, F. X. (1997b). Toward a pathophysiology of Attention-Deficit/Hyperactivity Disorder. *Clinical Pediatrics*, 1–13.

Castellanos, F. X., Giedd, J. N., Eckburg, P., Marsh, W. L., Vaituzis, A. C., Kaysen, D., Hamburger, S. D., & Rapoport, J. L. (1994). Quantitative morphology of the caudate nucleus in Attention Deficit Hyperactivity Disorder. *American Journal of Psychiatry, 151*(12), 1791–1796.

Castellanos, F. X., Giedd, J. N., Marsh, W. L., Hamburger, S. D., Vaituzis. A. C., Dickstein, D. P., Sarfatti, S., Vauss, Y., Snell, J., Lange, N., Kaysen, D., Krain, A. L., Ritchie, G. F., Rajapakse, J. C., & Rapoport, J. L. (1996). Quantitative brain magnetic resonance imaging in Attention Deficit/Hyperactivity Disorder. *Archives of General Psychiatry, 53*, 607–616.

Cook, E. H., Stein, M., Krasowski, M., Cox, N., Olkon, D., Kieffer, J., & Leventhal, B. (1995). Association of Attention-Deficit Disorder and the dopamine transporter gene. *American Journal of Human Genetics, 56*, 993–998.

Diller, L., Tanner, J. L., & Weil, J. (1996). Etiology of AD/HD: Nature or nurture? [Letter to the editor]. *American Journal of Psychiatry, 153*(3), 451–452.

Ernst, M. (1996). Neuroimaging in Attention-Deficit/Hyperactivity Disorder. In G. R. Lyon & J. M. Rumsey (Eds.), *Neuroimaging* (pp. 95–117). Baltimore, MD: Paul H. Brookes Publishing Company.

Faraone, S., Biederman, J., Chen, W., Milberger, S., Warburton, R., & Tsuang, M. (1995). Genetic heterogeneity in Attention-Deficit Hyperactivity Disorder (AD/HD): Gender, psychiatric comobidity, and maternal AD/HD. *Journal of Abnormal Psychology, 104*(2), 334–345.

Gaub, M., & Carlson, C. L. (1997). Gender differences in AD/HD: A meta-analysis and critical review. *Journal of American Academy of Child and Adolescent Psychiatry, 36*(8), 1036–1045.

Gross, M., Tofanelli, R., Butzirus, S., & Snodgrass, E. (1987). The effect of diets rich in and free from additives on the behavior of children with hyperkinetic and learning disorders. *Journal of American Academy of Child and Adolescent Psychiatry, 26*(1), 53–55.

Hauser, P., Zametkin, A., Martinez, P., Vitiello, B., Matochik, J., Mixson, A. J., & Weintraub, B. (1993). Attention-Deficit Hyperactivity Disorder in people with generalized resistance to thyroid hormone. *The New England Journal of Medicine, 328*(14), 997–1000.

Lefrancois, G. R. (1996). *The lifespan*. Belmont, CA: Wadsworth Publishing Company.

Lyon, G. R., & Rumsey, J. M. (Eds.). (1996). *Neuroimaging*. Baltimore: Paul H. Brookes Publishing Company.

Lyoo, K., Noam, G. G., Lee, C. K., Lee, H. K., Kennedy, B. P., & Renshaw, P. F. (1996). The corpus callosum and lateral ventricles in children with Attention Deficit/Hyperactivity Disorder: A brain magnetic resonance imaging study. *Biological Psychology, 40*, 1060–1063.

Mattes, J., & Gittelman, R. (1981). Effects of artificial food colorings in children with hyperactive symptoms. *Archives of General Psychiatry, 38*, 714–718.

Merriam-Webster's collegiate dictionary (9th ed.). (1987). Springfield, MA: Merriam-Webster.

Milberger, S., Biederman, J., Faraone, S., Chen, L., & Jones, J. (1996, September). Is maternal smoking during pregnancy a risk factor for Attention Deficit/Hyperactivity Disorder in children? *American Journal of Psychiatry, 153*(9), 1138–1142.

Stevens, L. J., Zentall, S. S., Deck, J. L., Abate, M. L., Watkins, B. A., Lipp, S. R., & Burgess, J. R. (1995). Essential fatty acid metabolism in boys with Attention-Deficit/Hyperactivity Disorder. *American Journal of Clinical Nutrition, 62*, 761–768.

Turnbull, A., Turnbull, H., Shank, M., & Leal, D. (1995). *Exceptional lives*. Upper Saddle River, NJ: Prentice-Hall.

Whitaker, A., Van Rossem, R., Feldman, J., Schonfeld, S., Pinto-Martin, J., Torre, C., Shaffer, D., & Paneth, N. (1997). Psychiatric outcomes in low-birth-weight children at age 6 years: Relation to neonatal cranial ultrasound abnormalities. *Archives of General Psychiatry, 54*, 847–856.

Studies on the Comorbidity of Attention Deficit/Hyperactivity Disorder with Other Disorders

We must not cease from exploration and the end of all our exploring will be to arrive where we began and to know the place for the first time.

—T. S. Eliot

There appear to be specific "subtypes" of Attention Deficit/Hyperactivity Disorder (AD/HD) that are defined by the co-occurrence or comorbidity with other disorders. These comorbid "subtypes" are not the same as the subtypes defined in the *Diagnostic and Statistical Manual of Mental Disorders*, fourth edition (*DSM-IV*) under AD/HD (see Appendix A). The apparent variety of subtypes contributes to the heterogeneity of the disorder, making it difficult to approach as a single entity. As educators we are accustomed to differentiating instruction to meet the individual needs of students based on learning styles. Therefore, information about subtypes is essential for educators if we are to truly understand the disorder and be able to modify our instruction accordingly, as we are already doing to accommodate the diverse styles of all learners. We must move beyond the misconception that AD/HD is a simple, homogeneous disorder; the research indicates that it is otherwise in many cases.

This chapter is a review of the research on the co-occurrence of AD/HD and other disorders, including: Conduct Disorder (CD), Oppositional Defiant Disorder (ODD), Learning Disabilities, Bipolar Disorder, Major Depressive Disorder, Anxiety Disorder, and Tourette's Syndrome. The frequency of co-occurrence of other disorders with AD/HD influenced the selection of comorbidity studies. The frequency of co-occurrence is highest for CD and ODD, followed by Learning Disabilities, then affective disorders (e.g., Major Depressive Disorder, Bipolar Disorder, Mood Disorder, and Anxiety Disorder), and Tourette's Syndrome with the lowest frequency of comorbidity (Barkley, 1997; Biederman, Newcorn, & Sprich, 1991). Allergies have been found to co-occur with AD/HD and research is reviewed to explore an association between the two conditions.

If there are "subtypes" of the disorder that are defined by comorbidity, then as educators we need to be aware of these differences and the impact this may have on the selection of instructional approaches. Just as with learning style preferences, first we need to be able to identify the various subtypes of AD/HD in order to develop meaningful interventions. In Chapter 5, I review research on intervention strategies that should enhance effectiveness in addressing the individual needs of students with AD/HD.

An additional benefit to the correct identification of subtypes is that it may enable us to implement preventive strategies. Research indicates that siblings of individuals with AD/HD are at a greater risk of developing associated disorders (Faraone et al., 1996). If, as members of an educational team, we can identify not only the subtype, but also the risk factors for siblings, we may be able to at least ameliorate the symptoms in subsequent students.

When studying comorbidity, it is important to keep in mind that we are not just looking at the random occurrence of two conditions. We must consider if the frequency of their occurrence together is greater than the occurrence of either alone. Peter S. Jensen, David Martin, and Dennis P. Cantwell (1997) use the example of an individual having a broken arm and a broken leg, which we would not necessarily consider to be a new syndrome unless it was the result of a specific set of risk factors, or if we could glean some meaningful treatment information from the co-occurrence of the two broken bones; in which case the two fractures may be classified under the Battered Child Syndrome. "It is this *synergism*, i.e., the interaction of the two or more conditions that conveys unique information, that should set the standard for determining whether the comorbid pattern should be regarded as a unique syndrome" (p.1067). It is this "standard" that defines comorbidity in the context that it is used in regard to AD/HD and consequent subtype identification.

In this chapter I provide an overview of the types of disorders that occur along with AD/HD and the frequency of their co-occurrence. The first two studies are reviews of literature on comorbidity of other disorders with AD/HD. The third is a longitudinal study, and there are four studies of patterns of comorbidity with specific disorders. The comorbidity of AD/HD with allergies is the focus of the eighth study. Although allergies are not in the same category as psychiatric disorders, their comorbidity is included as a confounding factor with AD/HD. A school-based study (conducted in a setting familar to teachers) is also included. These studies were selected to give educators a sense of the complexity of the disorder, which is due in part to comorbidity with other disorders.

REVIEW OF LITERATURE ON COMORBIDITY

1. Comorbidity in AD/HD: Implications for Research, Practice, and *DSM-V*. Peter S. Jensen, David Martin, and Dennis P. Cantwell. (1997). *Journal of American Academy of Child and Adolescent Psychiatry*, 36(8), 1065–1079.

This study consisted of a review of approximately 60 studies on AD/HD over the past 15 years to see if any patterns of comorbidity emerged and to see if these patterns shed some light on the nature and treatment of subtypes.[1] Such information might also serve as a means of predicting and thus preventing the full-blown manifestation of the disorder(s). The authors noted the significance of identifying subtypes based on comorbidity as a precursor to intervention. They further suggested that only through such classifications can we begin to approach subtypes as more homogeneous groups that may respond uniquely to various treatments and have different outcomes. *An analogy for the classroom might be using a predominantly visual mode of instruction for all students when auditory instruction might be better suited to some students.*

Results

The authors found the greatest amount of literature on comorbidity of AD/HD with CD/aggression (see Appendix C for *DSM-IV* definition). The following categories of factors were designated by the authors and taken directly from the article.

Demographic Factors

- Teenagers with AD/HD combined with CD or ODD (see Appendix D for *DSM-IV* definition) had the highest incidence of negative driving consequences.
- Hyperactivity was the greatest risk factor for school failure, and comorbidity with CD did not seem to increase this risk. The authors hypothesized that this may be due to the fact that school failure depends on intellectual performance rather than antisocial behavior.
- AD/HD plus CD doubled the risk of suspension and is the primary factor in higher expulsion and drop out rate over hyperactivity alone.
- AD/HD was a predictor of academic difficulties among subjects with the same I.Q.s.

Biological Factors

- There were higher rates of Attention Deficit Disorder (ADD) among delinquents compared to nondelinquents.
- Delinquents with ADD had greater verbal skill impairments and cognitive deficits than nondelinquents.

The risk factors identified for delinquency included ADD with neuropsychological deficits, aggressive behavior with early onset, and adversity in the home/family setting.

Family Genetic and Environmental Factors

- AD/HD appeared to be related to genetic factors, whereas aggression seemed to be more environmentally influenced.
- The development of Antisocial Personality Disorder (diagnosed only in individuals over 18 years of age [APA, 1994]) seemed to be influenced more by a history of adoptive family psychiatric problems and aggression than by the presence of AD/HD.
- It appears that the interaction between genetics and environment (i.e., family dynamics) must be considered as a risk factor for AD/HD with Antisocial Personality Disorder.
- Comorbidity of AD/HD with ODD (see Appendix D for APA definition) indicated a more negative outcome than AD/HD alone.

Clinical Course

- Comorbidity of AD/HD with CD had more severe, negative, and persistent outcomes than AD/HD alone.

AD/HD with Depression or Anxiety Disorders

- There was a greater prevalence of AD/HD in depressed children.
- The combination was more likely in younger children.
- Mothers of children with AD/HD and Depressive or Anxiety Disorders reported more symptoms for themselves than mothers of children with just AD/HD.
- Subjects with AD/HD and Anxiety Disorder responded less favorably to methylphenidate (e.g., Ritalin) than other AD/HD subjects, and in some cases the stimulant actually exacerbated the symptoms.
- Better response has been noted with the use of antidepressants than with methylphenidate.

AD/HD *with Learning Disabilities*

- Differentiation between the two indicated that although they have a high incidence of co-occurrence they are two distinct disorders.
- Learning Disability (LD) was characterized by deficits in word finding and linguistic fluency (reading disability).
- AD/HD reflected weaknesses in verbal learning and attention.

In conclusion, the combination of two or more disorders appeared to increase the severity of the symptoms and the likelihood of negative outcomes. Even though there was some contradiction among research findings, the authors were inclined to believe that, particularly in the case of AD/HD with CD, there was a synergistic effect, which suggested a distinct subtype. *There were implications embedded in this review that apply to the educational setting summarized as follows.*

AD/HD *and CD*

- Lower I.Q.s
- More reading and learning difficulties
- Multimodal treatment indicated (behavioral and pharmacological therapies)

AD/HD *and Anxiety Disorder*

- Inhibition of attentional processing tasks
- Lower levels of externalizing behaviors
- Unique pharmacological considerations
- Direct instruction of academic skills is most beneficial

Early intervention for children identified with AD/HD may prevent the development of comorbid conditions that may be responsible for later academic and social problems.

2. **Comorbidity of Attention Deficit Hyperactivity Disorder with Conduct, Depressive, Anxiety, and Other Disorders.** Joseph Biederman, Jeffrey Newcorn, and Susan Sprich. (1991). *American Journal of Psychiatry, 148(5), 564–577.*

This study was a review of the literature on comorbidity with AD/HD. It was conducted to determine what research has been done and what the findings indicated regarding the co-occurrence of other disorders along with AD/HD.

Summary of Review

Comorbid Condition	Findings
1. Conduct Disorder	• co-occurrence with AD/HD in 30–50% of cases
2. Oppositional Defiant Disorder	• limited research • frequently combined with CD
3. Mood Disorders	• across studies found 15–75% co-occurrence with AD/HD • vulnerability and risks shared within families • either disorder alone has implications for negative outcomes, outcomes are greater with comorbidity
4. Anxiety Disorders	• about 25% co-occurrence with AD/HD • higher incidence of AD/HD in offspring of parents with Anxiety Disorder • research indicates that although these two disorders co-occur and have a high occurrence within families, they appear to be transmitted independently
5. Learning Disabilities	• 10–92% reported co-occurrence with AD/HD • difficult to distinguish between the two
6. Other Disorders: Mental Retardation Tourette's Syndrome	• AD/HD is 3 to 4 times more prevalent in this population than in the general population • high incidence of CD • about 60% of youth with Tourette's also have AD/HD • conversely, only a small percentage of youth with AD/HD have Tourette's • debate exists over whether AD/HD and Tourette's are genetically linked • stimulant medication for AD/HD is not advisable for youth at risk for Tourette's Syndrome

The authors suggested the literature delineated patterns of comorbidity that had implications for treatment and intervention that were appropriate for the combined disorders and varied from those indicated for individually occurring disorders.

LONGITUDINAL STUDY OF COMORBIDITY WITH AD/HD

3. **A Prospective 4-Year Follow-up Study of Attention Deficit Hyperactivity and Related Disorders.** Joseph Biederman, Stephen Faraone, Sharon Milberger, Jessica Guite, Eric Mick, Lisa Chen, Douglas Mennin, Abbe Marrs, Cheryl Ouellete, Phoebe Moore, Thomas Spencer, Dennis Norman, Timothy Wilens, Ilana Kraus, and James Perrin. (1996). *Archives of General Psychiatry, 53*, 437–446.

For individuals with AD/HD adolescence and young adulthood usually present increased academic, social, and emotional problems. The frequent co-occurrence of AD/HD with other disorders makes it difficult to determine whether the negative outcomes are due to the AD/HD, the other disorder, or the combination. In an attempt to predict outcomes based on specific disorders in combination with AD/HD, Joseph Biederman and colleagues studied two groups of boys between 6 and 17 years of age. One group of subjects was identified with AD/HD; the control group consisted of normal subjects. They conducted the study over a period of four years. The subjects were all evaluated in five areas of functioning (social, family, cognitive, achievement, and school) in addition to psychiatric disorder, *making this research of particular interest to teachers and parents.* A baseline was established for all subjects for the presence of comorbid disorders in order to determine if these comorbidities would persist and were not just secondary effects of the AD/HD.

Results

Baseline Comorbidity	*Predicted Risk*
1. Conduct Disorder	• Conduct Disorder (to persist) • Oppositional Defiant Disorder • Bipolar Disorder (Manic-Depressive) • Alcohol and drug dependence
2. Major Depression	• Oppositional Defiant Disorder • Major Depression (to persist) • Bipolar Disorder • Agoraphobia (fear of public places)
3. Multiple Anxiety Disorder	• Anxiety disorders
4. AD/HD without any other disorders (compared to non-AD/HD)	• Oppositional Defiant Disorder • Tic disorders • Language disorders
5. AD/HD comorbid with any other disorders (compared to pure AD/HD and non-AD/HD controls)	• greater family conflict • poorer family interactions and cohesiveness

Poor social outcomes such as delinquency, substance abuse, and antisocial behavior were attributable to the comorbid disorders rather than the AD/HD alone. However, the AD/HD appeared to be responsible for cognitive and academic deficits as evidenced by repeating grades, LD diagnosis, need for academic tutoring, and placement in special classes. *The distinction between characteristics associated with AD/HD versus those of the comorbid disorders explains a great deal of what we see in classrooms with AD/HD students. Such students have academic problems that are exacerbated by behavior problems that are the result of the comorbid disorder(s).*

If we can recognize the unique characteristics of the specific subtypes, we can adjust our interventions accordingly. Educators must begin looking at students with AD/HD from a multifaceted perspective if we hope to be successful, or, more importantly, if we want our students to experience success in their lives.

COMPARISON STUDY OF *DSM-IV* SUBTYPES

4. **Patterns of Comorbidity Associated with Subtypes of Attention-Deficit/Hyperactivity Disorder among 6- to 12-Year-Old Children.** Ricardo Eiraldi, Thomas Power, and Christine Maguth Nezu. (1997). *Journal of American Academy of Child and Adolescent Psychiatry, 36*(4), 503–514.

DSM-IV defines AD/HD as three types: Predominantly Inattentive, Predominantly Impulsive-Hyperactive, and Combined Type (APA, 1994) (see Appendix A). In general, the Inattentive Type would be associated with more internalizing behaviors, whereas the Impulsive-Hyperactive Type is more likely to be manifested through more overt, external behaviors. Ricardo Eiraldi, Thomas Power, and Christine Maguth Nezu studied comorbidity patterns of AD/HD using the Inattentive and Combined Type categories, as defined by *DSM-IV*, and a normal control group. Subjects were assigned to categories on the basis of structured interviews and parent and teacher ratings.

Subjects in the AD/HD Combined Type category had I.Q. scores significantly lower than those in the control group. Socioeconomic status (SES) was also lower for the AD/HD Combined group compared to the AD/HD Inattentive Type and the control group. As the authors hypothesized, the co-occurrence of disorders with externalizing behaviors was significantly more prevalent among subjects with AD/HD Combined Type than among subjects in the other subtypes. Specifically, CD and ODD had a much higher incidence in the AD/HD Combined Type group than in the AD/HD Inattentive Type group.

Although externalizing behaviors were less evident in the Inattentive group in school settings, children in this group were reported to have more conduct problems at home than those in the control group. The authors suggested that this may be because their behaviors (e.g., forgetfulness, disorganization) are less tolerable in the home setting, causing conflict with parents. Both AD/HD groups were at equal risk for internalizing disorders such as anxiety or depression.

MAJOR DEPRESSION

5. **Psychiatric Comorbidity among Referred Juveniles with Major Depression: Fact or Artifact?** Joseph Biederman, Stephen Faraone, Eric Mick,

and Elise Lelon. (1995). *Journal of American Academy of Child and Adolescent Psychiatry, 34*(5), 579–590.

There is a high incidence of juvenile depression and comorbid disorders, which raises questions regarding the nature of the combined disorders. Within a sample group of clinically referred children and adolescents, 40% met the criteria for a diagnosis of Major Depression. Many were also diagnosed with AD/HD, CD, and Anxiety Disorder. The authors found that the onset of these co-occurring disorders, in most cases, predated that of the Major Depression by a number of years, indicating that they may be distinct disorders with overlapping symptoms.

The implication of this finding is that it is important to diagnose all co-occurring disorders as the treatment may be different for each. The example given was that of a specialist in AD/HD who may attribute symptoms to the AD/HD, thus missing the dual diagnosis of Major Depression; a clinician specializing in Major Depression may overlook the AD/HD symptoms. The treatment procedures differ for these two disorders; therefore, it is important to recognize both, as well as the interaction between them. Teachers and parents see irritability as one of the predominant characteristics that prompt them to refer depressed children.

BIPOLAR DISORDER

6. **Mania-like Symptoms Suggestive of Childhood-onset Bipolar Disorder in Clinically Referred Children.** Janet Wozniak, Joseph Biederman, Kathleen Kiely, J. Stuart Ablon, Stephen Faraone, Elizabeth Mundy, and Douglas Mennin. (1995). *Journal of American Academy of Child and Adolescent Psychiatry, 34*(7), 867–876.

Definition of Terms

Bipolar (affective) Disorder: a psychotic disorder characterized by alternating periods of mania and mental depression; manic-depressive illness: now the preferred term in psychiatry (*Webster's*, 1997, p.141)

Mania: excitement manifested by mental and physical hyperactivity, disorganization of behavior and elevation of mood (*Merriam-Webster's*, 1987, p.723)

Through a review of the literature over the years, cases of childhood onset of Bipolar Disorder have been cited, yet the report of incidence is extremely low. In more recent years there has been an increase in the number of cases documented. One of the complications involved in establishing the frequency of occurrence of Bipolar Disorder in children is the manner in which it presents itself. In young children the disorder manifests as irritability, aggression, and temper outbursts, which may be misdiagnosed as depression. Euphoria occurs in older children and adults with Bipolar Disorder.

The characteristic behaviors of Bipolar Disorder overlap with those of AD/HD, including impulsivity, distractibility, emotional lability (mood swings), and hyperactivity. The comorbidity of these two disorders is high, as was hypothesized and then demonstrated in this study. Of the 43 manic subjects included in this study, all but one also met the criteria for AD/HD. Bipolar subjects who were also diagnosed AD/HD had significantly more AD/HD characteristics than those that were only diagnosed with AD/HD.

Educators need to be aware of the symptoms of childhood Bipolar Disorder, the frequency of comorbidity with AD/HD, and how the combination presents itself. As the authors state, more research needs to be done to determine what the interaction is between these two disorders and the behavioral manifestations in the home and educational settings.

PARENT-CHILD INTERACTIONS

7. **Parent Characteristics and Parent-child Interactions in Families of Non-problem Children and AD/HD Children with Higher and Lower Levels of Oppositional-defiant Behavior.** Charlotte Johnston. (1996). *Journal of Abnormal Child Psychology, 24*(1), 85–104.

As the title indicates, the focus of this study was on the interactions between parents and children, some without AD/HD and others with AD/HD comorbid with low and high levels of oppositional defiant behaviors. The children were given tasks to perform, some academic in nature and of varying levels of interest. Parent-child interactions were observed across tasks. In high interest tasks, there was less need for parental intervention; therefore, less conflict occurred between the parents and children. There was no notable difference in parent-child interaction among the three groups (i.e., without AD/HD, with AD/HD, and AD/HD comorbid with oppositional defiant behaviors) during academic tasks. High interest appears to be a positive factor for student compliance. *This lends support to the current thrust in education toward the use of high-interest, real-life activities for all students, especially those with AD/HD.*

Results

• Behavior problems were greatest in the AD/HD group with high oppositional defiant behaviors.

• Parent behaviors were *observed* to be the same across all groups.

- Parents of both AD/HD groups were *reported* to use more negative and reactive strategies than parents of the control group.
- Fathers of AD/HD subjects with high oppositional defiant behavior had a greater incidence of psychological disturbance than those of non-AD/HD subjects.
- There was a greater divorce/separation rate among parents of AD/HD children with oppositional defiant behaviors.

There were differences in parenting styles used with all AD/HD children compared to non-AD/HD subjects.

ALLERGIES AND AD/HD

8. **Coincidence of Attention Deficit Disorder and Atopic Disorders in Children: Empirical Findings and Hypothetical Background.** Norbet Roth, Jutta Beyreiss, Klaus Schlenzka, and Hannelore Beyer. (1991). *Journal of Abnormal Child Psychology, 19*(1), 1–13.

Definition of Terms

atopic: a probably hereditary allergy characterized by symptoms (as asthma, hay fever, or hives) produced upon exposure to the exciting antigen without inoculation (*Merriam-Webster's*, 1987, p.113)

catecholamine: any of various amines (as epinephrine, norepinephrine, and dopamine) that function as hormones or neurotransmitters or both (*Merriam-Webster's*, 1987, p.215)

Over the years there have been reports of the co-occurrence of allergies in individuals with AD/HD, indicating that there may be a relationship between the two conditions. There appears to be some overlap in the neurotransmitters involved in the nervous system (operant in behavior problems) and the immune system (involved with allergies). *I have observed a number of students who were diagnosed with AD/HD and allergies, which caused me to wonder if there was some connection between the two or at least an interaction between medications used in the treatment of each.*

If there is a relationship between allergies and AD/HD, then a random sample of subjects with allergies should have a higher percentage of AD/HD diagnoses. This was the hypothesis that Norbet Roth and colleagues examined. Two groups were compared, one comprised of children with allergies and a control group of children without allergies. The procedure for gathering data included the administration of a series of psychomotor tests, parent ratings, and developmental histories.

Results

- Younger children had higher hyperactivity ratings in both groups.
- There were no significant differences by gender in identification of AD/HD.
- There were no significant differences in identification of AD/HD due to parental level of education or occupation.
- A significantly higher number of subjects with allergies exhibited characteristics of ADD than controls.
- Children with allergies appeared to have greater difficulty adjusting processing strategies to match changing task demands.

Future research needs to be done regarding individuals with allergies and AD/HD to see if this is indeed a subgroup with specific characteristics and considerations. *It would be interesting to know how many teachers have observed the combination of these two disorders or conditions in students in their classrooms.*

Unfortunately, I was only able to find one additional study dealing with the co-occurrence of allergies with AD/HD, although the mention of such a relationship is made in other research. The second study was longitudinal and conducted on a large sample of children drawn from the general population. The researchers did not find an association between allergic disorders and AD/HD behaviors as reported by parents, teachers and the children themselves (McGee, Stanton, & Sears, 1993). The differences in subjects may account for some of the differences in the findings. Roth et al. used children who were clinically referred for allergy disorders and a nonclinical control group; McGee et al. used children from the general population.

SCHOOL-BASED PREVENTION PROGRAM

9. **Prevalence of AD/HD and Comorbid Disorders among Elementary School Children Screened for Disruptive Behavior.** Gerald August, George Realmuto, Angus W. MacDonald III, Sean Nugent, and Ross Crosby. (1996). *Journal of Abnormal Child Psychology, 24*(5), 571–595.

The parameters of this study are unique in that it was conducted as part of a school-based prevention program for conduct disorders. The majority of other research has been done with clinically referred subjects for purely research purposes. This study included a prevention component based on the identification of risk factors associated with comorbidity and parental characteristics of children presenting disruptive behaviors. One limitation of so many studies has been that, due to the clinical nature of the subjects, the results cannot be generalized to the larger school population. This research was conducted in a school setting making the results more relevant to school personnel. However, the authors noted that the subjects, 318 students in grades 1 through 4 who screened positive for disruptive behavior, primarily represented suburban, middle-class, white populations and, therefore, did not address the added risks associated with economic disadvantage.

Results

- Almost 66% of the subjects met the *DSM-IV* criteria for AD/HD.
- Many had comorbidity with other psychiatric disorders, primarily ODD (see Appendix D for *DSM-IV* definition) and CD (see Appendix C for *DSM-IV* definition).
- ODD or CD did not occur frequently without AD/HD.
- There was a lower comorbidity with CD in this study than with samples from higher risk populations.[2]
- Since students were screened for disruptive behavior, those with primarily internalizing behaviors (i.e., inattentive subtype of AD/HD) were indirectly excluded.

The authors believe that by identifying patterns of comorbidity, early intervention programs may be implemented to prevent the full-blown manifestation of CD and ODD in high-risk populations.

CHAPTER SUMMARY

The nine studies reviewed in this chapter represent a sample of the research being done on comorbidity of other disorders with AD/HD. The first two studies included extensive reviews of the findings in this area. As with all the research being examined on AD/HD, this is just the tip of the iceberg. The more we learn the more we realize how little we know, but only through such a review can we hope to glean some understanding of the disorder(s). The following summary of findings (Table 3.1) from this chapter should provide a quick reference for educators. It is not intended to serve as a substitute for reading the entire chapter as there is so much more to be gained from reading the results in the context of each study.

It is imperative that educators have a basic understanding of the significant role that comorbidity plays in the expression and dynamics of AD/HD as a precursor to intervention. The findings reviewed in this chapter lay the foundation for the selection and development of appropriate intervention strategies. Without an awareness of how various co-occurring disorders interact, teachers are less likely to plan and implement effective techniques

Table 3.1
Summary of Results for Comorbidity with AD/HD

Study	Findings	Implications
1. Review of literature on comorbidity over 15 years	• comorbidity intensifies severity of outcomes	• prevention of comorbid condition through recognition of characteristics and predicted risks
2. Review of literature	• identifies patterns of comorbidity	• specific interventions based on patterns of comorbidity • combinations may respond differently than individual disorders
3. Longitudinal study	• established predicted risks for comorbidity	• results indicate specific educational outcomes • need to approach AD/HD from a new perspective

AD/HD Comorbid with Other Disorders

Study	Findings	Implications
4. Comparison study of two *DSM-IV* subtypes of AD/HD with control without AD/HD	• AD/HD Combined type had lower I.Q. and SES than controls • higher incidence of Conduct Disorder and Oppositional Defiance Disorder with Combined Type	• inattentive group has more conflict at home than at school • Combined Type more prone to acting out, externalizing behavior at school
5. Comorbidity with Major Depression	• AD/HD and Major Depression may be distinct disorders with overlapping symptoms • Many comorbid for Conduct Disorder, AD/HD, and Anxiety Disorder along with Major Depression	• awareness of co-occurrence as well as symptoms of individual disorders as basis for intervention selection • irritability is trait causing many referrals of children with depression
6. Comorbidity with Bipolar Disorder	• overlap of symptoms, which may cause misdiagnosis	• awareness of frequency of comorbidity • awareness of symptoms of Bipolar Disorder • awareness of possible interactions between the two disorders

Table 3.1 (*continued*)

Study	Findings	Implications
7. Comorbidity with Oppositional Defiance Disorder (focus on parent-child interactions)	• oppositional defiant behaviors with AD/HD compounds the disorder	• emphasizes value of high interest academic tasks for all children and especially those with AD/HD
8. Allergies and AD/HD	• higher hyperactivity rating for *all* younger children • higher incidence of AD/HD in allergy group	• awareness of possible co-occurrence of AD/HD with allergies • higher than average co-occurrence of AD/HD in this group
9. School-based prevention program with focus on Conduct Disorder	• 2/3 of disruptive students met AD/HD criteria • high comorbidity of Conduct Disorder and Oppositional Defiant Disorder with AD/HD	• emphasizes importance of early identification and intervention as prevention

for students with AD/HD. Although no one would question the need for additional research on comorbidity, enough information already exists for us to make wiser decisions in our classrooms. In addition, knowledge of risk factors and predictors can be used to enhance our ability to prevent future academic and behavioral problems in our classrooms by providing early intervention.

NOTES

1. Since this review was conducted on literature from over a 15 year period, the definitions and terms may vary. In order to maintain the integrity of the original studies, the terms in this review are consistent with those sources. Therefore, Attention Deficit Disorder (ADD) may be used instead of AD/HD, and the reader is reminded that the defining characteristics may vary somewhat depending on the date of the studies.

2. Risk factors have been defined in previous chapters. Some examples are maternal smoking during pregnancy, family history of AD/HD and other psychiatric disorders, generalized resistance to thyroid hormone, and low-birth-weight.

REFERENCES

American Psychiatric Association (APA). (1994). *Diagnostic and statistical manual of mental disorders* (4th ed.). Washington, DC: Author.

August, G., Realmuto, G., MacDonald III, A. W., Nugent, S., & Crosby, R. (1996). Prevalence of AD/HD and comorbid disorders among elementary school children screened for disruptive behavior. *Journal of Abnormal Child Psychology, 24*(5), 571–595.

Barkley, R. A. (1997). *ADHD and the nature of self-control*. New York: Guilford Press.

Biederman, J., Faraone, S., Mick, E., & Lelon, E. (1995). Psychiatric comorbidity among referred juveniles with Major Depression: Fact or artifact? *Journal of American Academy of Child and Adolescent Psychiatry, 34*(5), 579–590.

Biederman, J., Faraone, S., Milberger, S., Guite, J., Mick, E., Chen, L., Mennin, D., Marrs, A., Ouellete, C., Moore, P., Spencer, T., Norman, D., Wilens, T., Kraus, I., & Perrin, J. (1996). A prospective 4-year follow-up study of Attention Deficit Hyperactivity and related disorders. *Archives of General Psychiatry, 53*, 437–446.

Biederman, J., Newcorn, J., & Sprich, S. (1991). Comorbidity of Attention Deficit Hyperactivity Disorder with Conduct, Depressive, Anxiety, and other disorders. *American Journal of Psychiatry, 148*(5), 564–577.

Eiraldi, R., Power, T., & Nezu, C. M. (1997). Patterns of comorbidity associated with subtypes of Attention-Deficit/Hyperactivity Disorder among 6- to 12-year-old children. *Journal of American Academy of Child and Adolescent Psychiatry, 36*(4), 503–514.

Faraone, S., Biederman, J., Mennin, D., Gershon, J., & Tsuang, M. (1996). A prospective follow-up study of children at risk for AD/HD: Psychiatric, neurological, and psychosocial outcome. *Journal of Child and Adolescent Psychiatry, 35*(11), 1449–1459.

Jensen, P. S., Martin, D., & Cantwell, D. P. (1997). Comorbidity in AD/HD: Implications for research, practice, and *DSM-V*. *Journal of American Academy of Child and Adolescent Psychiatry, 36*(8), 1065–1079.

Johnston, C. (1996). Parent characteristics and parent-child interactions in families of nonproblem children and AD/HD children with higher and lower levels of oppositional-defiant behavior. *Journal of Abnormal Child Psychology, 24*(1), 85–104.

McGee, R., Stanton, W. R., & Sears, M. R. (1993). Allergic disorders and Attention Deficit Disorder in children. *Journal of Abnormal Child Psychology, 21*(1), 79–88.

Merriam-Webster's collegiate dictionary (9th ed.). (1987). Springfield, MA: Merriam-Webster.

Roth, N., Beyreiss, J., Schlenzka, K., & Beyer, H. (1991). Coincidence of Attention Deficit Disorder and atopic disorders in children: Empirical findings and hypothetical background. *Journal of Abnormal Child Psychology, 19*(1), 1–13.

Webster's new world college dictionary (3rd ed.). (1997). New York: Simon & Schuster.

Wozniak, J., Biederman, J., Kiely, K., Ablon, J. S., Faraone, S., Mundy, E., & Mennin, D. (1995). Mania-like symptoms suggestive of childhood-onset Bipolar Disorder in clinically referred children. *Journal of American Academy of Child and Adolescent Psychiatry, 34*(7), 867–876.

Studies on the Diagnosis of Attention Deficit/Hyperactivity Disorder

Yet with all this abounding experience, this deity known, I shall dare
to discover some province, some gift of my own.
—Robert Browning

Parents entrust us with their most precious possession, their children. When
problems develop that we have been led to believe are beyond our ability
to deal with, we either refer them to other professionals or just fail to
provide any support, as is often the case with Attention Deficit/
Hyperactivity Disorder (AD/HD). AD/HD has typically been defined
through a medical model, and therefore, diagnosed by a medical doctor. In
fact, teachers have been cautioned against even suggesting to a parent that
a child may have AD/HD. As a result, teachers unintentionally broaden the
communication gap between themselves and parents of children exhibiting
AD/HD characteristics. At a time when parents need our support and guidance the most, we are unable to give it.

It is not our place to diagnose a child with AD/HD, but it is our job to
identify specific academic and social difficulties displayed by any of our
students. Only through a thorough understanding of the risk factors identified in Chapters 2 and 3, under causes and comorbidity, can we prepare
ourselves to meet this challenge. There are many interventions that we can
put in place prior to a student being labeled AD/HD by a physician. Some
of these preintervention strategies may preclude the necessity of a formal
identification. After all, the primary value in a label is the services or interventions that come as a result. Medication is only one possible intervention, and it should not be used as the only treatment. It would behoove

educators to move beyond the misconception that a medical diagnosis of AD/HD must come before classroom interventions are implemented. In the event that a student does require a formal diagnosis, educators can maintain the faith and goodwill of parents by "doing something" to help in the meantime, while at the same time providing advice on how to seek additional professional help.

Education is a caring profession. Armed with the right information, teachers can earn the respect and support they deserve from the parents of all their students. It is essential that teachers know the current diagnostic procedures for AD/HD. They play a crucial role in that diagnosis; they often are the first to identify a problem; they implement interventions; they serve as primary sources of information to medical professionals; they make initial contacts with parents; and they serve as key members of the team designed to meet the special needs of these students. Although they may not be in the position to make an official diagnosis of AD/HD, teachers are a significant source of information to those professionals who do make that diagnosis.

OVERVIEW OF CURRENT DIAGNOSTIC PROCESS

As previously stated, the criteria for diagnosing AD/HD have been set by the American Psychiatric Association (APA) in the *Diagnostic and Statistical Manual of Mental Disorders*, which is in its fourth edition (*DSM-IV*, 1994) (see Appendix A). Presently, the identification of AD/HD is made on the basis of behavioral observations that are compared to the *DSM-IV* criteria. Data-gathering methods that are typically used include: parent and child interviews, parent and teacher rating scales, family and developmental histories, and a physical exam (Dulcan & Benson, 1997). In order to get a comprehensive picture, it is necessary to do a multifaceted assessment. Each component, outlined below, is significant and contributes to the larger picture.

Interviews

Parent interviews are used to obtain information about the family. This information should include family dynamics and demographic factors, as well as the occurrence of AD/HD or other psychiatric disorders in other family members (Dulcan & Benson, 1997). Parents may also be informative about persistent or troubling behaviors. Their recollections tend to be clearer than those of the AD/HD individuals themselves.

Teachers can provide information on academic performance and attendance. The classroom environment and the instructional style of the teacher may also be influential factors (Dulcan & Benson, 1997).

Rating Scales

Conners Parent and Teacher Rating Scales (probably familiar to most teachers) are among the most popular and frequently used scales for rating student behavior (Barkley, 1990). Rating scales should be completed by parents and all teachers who are involved with the student. It is important to have observational feedback across settings as AD/HD can be situational, yielding different results from teacher to teacher. AD/HD rating scales typically include items that measure a student's activity level, attending skills, degree of compliance, anger control, and ability to get along with others.

Medical Evaluation

Health care professionals can rule out confounding conditions that may mimic AD/HD. In addition to a physical examination, lab tests may be indicated to determine if the patient has lead intoxication, a thyroid disorder, or a zinc deficiency (Dulcan & Benson, 1997). A neurological assessment may help ascertain whether or not the individual has difficulty performing neurological tasks (Nemethy, 1997).

Comprehensive History

By recording prenatal development or complications and developmental milestones, it is often possible to identify risk factors associated with the development of AD/HD (Nemethy, 1997). For example, in Chapter 2 (Causes) specific risk factors are identified including maternal smoking (Milberger et al., 1996), low-birth-weight (LBW) (Breslau et al., 1996), and heredity (Biederman et al., 1992; Faraone et al., 1995). If a prenatal history reveals one or more of these indicators, then the individual is at higher risk for developing AD/HD (Nemethy, 1997). Although teachers are not usually involved in the development of a comprehensive medical history profile, it is useful to be aware of its significance. It may also shed some light on the behaviors we observe in the classroom.

The studies reviewed in this chapter relate to the diagnosis of AD/HD. The areas covered are diagnostic issues, diagnostic criteria (e.g., *DSM-IV*), and laboratory measures such as neuroimaging techniques (i.e., MRI, EEG) and lab tasks. This review takes us from where we are now to a look into the future.

DIAGNOSTIC ISSUES

The diagnostic issues addressed in this section deal with the influence of risk factors, the diagnosis of social disability, and the varying perceptions

among participants involved in the identification process of students with
AD/HD.

1. **A Prospective Four-Year Follow-up Study of Children at Risk for
   AD/HD: Psychiatric, Neuropsychological, and Psychosocial Outcome.**
   Stephen V. Faraone, Joseph Biederman, Douglas Mennin, Jonathan Ger-
   shon, and Ming T. Tsuang. (1996). *Journal of American Academy of
   Child and Adolescent Psychiatry, 35*(11), 1449–1459.

*As mentioned in the introduction to this chapter, if we can identify risk
factors for siblings of students with AD/HD, we may be able to implement
preventive interventions. As teachers know so well, if we can intervene
before a behavioral cycle is established, our efforts are more effective than
when we try to correct a problem after it has been established. This holds
true for behavioral and academic functions alike. In addition to using good
practices for all students, we can implement anticipatory and preventive
techniques for students at risk for AD/HD. An awareness of intervention
strategies is essential to this implementation.*

This study focused on the behavioral and academic outcomes that siblings of individuals with AD/HD are at risk for manifesting, including comorbid anxiety, conduct and learning disorders, school failure, and
indications of impaired intellectual functioning. All of the participants in
the study were assessed for AD/HD according to the *Diagnostic and Statistical Manual of Mental Disorders*, third edition, revised (*DSM-III-R*) criteria at the beginning of the study, after one year, and again after four
years. Three groups of subjects were included: children with AD/HD, normal controls, and the biological siblings of both of the other two groups.
Family histories were obtained at the first assessment. Intelligence testing
and psychiatric, cognitive and AD/HD assessments were conducted at the
baseline and at each follow-up session.

Results

- One-half of the siblings of AD/HD children had experienced some degree of
  school failure and one-fourth were diagnosed with AD/HD at the four-year assessment, suggesting that this is a high-risk group.
- A greater impairment existed in siblings of AD/HD children who were AD/HD
  themselves than in control siblings and non-AD/HD siblings in all domains evaluated.
- The non-AD/HD siblings of AD/HD children and the siblings of controls were
  more alike than dissimilar.
- Within the high-risk group (siblings of students with AD/HD), there were signif-

icant deficits in *arithmetic achievement, attention, and reading,* in addition to more repeated grades, tutoring, and special education services.

• The high-risk group showed only marginal deficits on intelligence tests, suggesting that school difficulties were not due to deficits in ability.

• Social difficulties were exhibited across settings (home and school) for the high-risk group.

• The degree of impairment and comorbidity of the AD/HD siblings reflected that of children with AD/HD who were clinically referred.

These findings provide a strong basis for establishing screening procedures for children in the high-risk group for AD/HD and other related problems. However, many of the target behaviors were not identified until the four-year follow-up, indicating a possible age factor. *Within a school setting, awareness of the increased familial risk for AD/HD can serve as justification for developing interventions before problems occur, as well as prior to a clinical diagnosis.*

2. **Toward a New Psychometric Definition of Social Disability in Children with Attention-Deficit Hyperactivity Disorder.** Ross W. Greene, Joseph Biederman, Stephen V. Faraone, Cheryl Ouellette, Courtney Penn, and Susan M. Griffin. (1996). *Journal of American Academy of Child and Adolescent Psychiatry, 35*(5), 571–578.

One area often associated with AD/HD is that of social deficits. Many children with AD/HD have difficulty getting along with others. The majority of the research on AD/HD focuses on cognitive and behavioral aspects. If social dysfunction puts an AD/HD student at even greater risk for poor outcomes, mechanisms need to be developed to identify social deficits. The authors propose the establishment of a process to diagnose social disabilities in children with AD/HD in much the same way that we diagnose learning disabilities. The procedure used in the study involved demonstrating a discrepancy between intelligence quotients derived from selected subtests on the Wechsler Intelligence Scale for Children–Revised (WISC-R) and social functioning as measured by the Social Adjustment Inventory for Children and Adolescents (SAICA).

As predicted, there were significantly higher numbers (22%) of children with AD/HD that were also diagnosed as socially disabled, compared to none in the control group of non-AD/HD subjects, when using the diagnostic approach described above. The consequences of such behaviors include peer rejection and poor relations with teachers and parents, which have a negative impact on self-esteem. In the long run, socially disabled students characteristically are more aggressive, experience more school failure, and are prone to substance abuse. Through early identification of a student at high risk for social disabilities, we may be able to avert or at least ameliorate the severe negative outcomes associated with it. This study puts forth a procedure for diagnosing social deficits and suggests that AD/HD plus social disability may be a distinct subtype of the disorder, in which case specific interventions are indicated. *In the meantime, while more research is being done to clarify this issue, teachers should be sensitive to the ramifications of concomitant social dysfunction in students with AD/HD and cognizant of possible early interventions.*

3. **Social Considerations in the Labeling of Students as Attention Deficit Hyperactivity Disordered.** Jack S. Damico and Lloyd E. Augustine. (1995). *Seminars in Speech and Language, 16(4), 259–271.*

The diagnosis of AD/HD is influenced by a number of variables. Through an examination of the steps in the identification of AD/HD one can gain a better understanding of the disorder and the varying perceptions of those involved. In addition there are often environmental factors that may contribute to the manifestation of AD/HD behaviors, which make it necessary to study this phenomenon in the environment in which it occurs. These researchers approached the study of the identification process through the use of in-depth interviews of all participants within the setting that it normally occurs.

The findings of this study are enlightening as they reveal the basis of a great deal of the miscommunication and misunderstanding that often develop among school personnel, parents, and nonschool professionals (i.e., physicians, psychologists) regarding the diagnosis of AD/HD. The authors reported seven major findings from their observations and interviews with people involved in the labeling process of students with AD/HD. The most significant finding was that of the varying perceptions among those closest to the issue of diagnosis and labeling of students with AD/HD.

Results

- Parents perceived teachers and other school personnel as unresponsive to their concerns about their children's difficulties, which led them to seek outside help (i.e., physician/psychologist).

- In most cases, upon the diagnosis of AD/HD, the physician recommended medication, and the parents were in agreement.

- After the physician's diagnosis of AD/HD, in over half of the cases the schools provided extra services or accommodations; in the remaining cases the schools initially resisted making accommodations; in one case a court hearing was pending.

- Interviews revealed a lack of belief in AD/HD as a disability category on the part of some school personnel.
- There was an overwhelming belief on the part of all participants in the survey that the diagnosis of AD/HD fell solely in the realm of medicine or psychiatry and must come from a physician (which led to division rather than collaboration).
- There was a pervasive reliance on the medical model to explain AD/HD and the belief that the disability was located entirely within the individual and could only be treated with medication.
- An adversarial relationship developed between parents and school personnel.
- Along with the label came the interventions the parents had asked for in the first place; the label yields power.
- The AD/HD label was a "no fault label" that placed the blame on something internal to the child and relieved the parents and teachers of the guilt of poor parenting or poor teaching.

The authors hope that educators will use these findings as an impetus to adjust their approach to children with AD/HD and consider the variety of environmental variables that come into play. *Teachers have many viable alternatives at their disposal if they are willing to recognize them and go beyond the limited thinking of the medical model with medication as the only intervention.*

Educators have the ability to reestablish good rapport with parents by valuing their input. We should put the "power" back in understanding and collaboration instead of in the "label." We do not need a diagnostic label to identify student difficulties and to put meaningful interventions in place. Regardless of the label, teachers need to be in touch with parents and students and focus on helping the child. The better that educators understand the youngster the more they can help. Our first and foremost responsibility is to our students and meeting their needs as only we can in the classroom. This is in fact what our profession dictates that we do.

DIAGNOSTIC CRITERIA

A number of factors may influence prevalence rates of AD/HD, including the current definition and diagnostic criteria being used and how they are interpreted. Over the years, revisions have been made to the *DSM* (see Appendix E). In this section, studies are reviewed that focus on changes in the diagnostic criteria and the resulting impact on diagnosis of AD/HD.

4. **Methodological Differences in the Diagnosis of Attention-Deficit Hyperactivity Disorder: Impact on Prevalence.** Morris J. Cohen, Cynthia A. Riccio, and José J. Gonzalez. (1994). *Journal of Emotional and Behavioral Disorders,* 2(1), 31–38.

Diagnosis has a direct impact on prevalence rates. If clinicians are using broad interpretations of the *DSM-IV* then the prevalence rates will be higher. In the United States, individuals with AD/HD and comorbid disorders are included along with those having AD/HD without comorbid disorders (pure AD/HD). As a result, the reported rate of AD/HD is higher in this country than in other countries such as the United Kingdom that consider only pure AD/HD in prevalence rates. In addition, in the United Kingdom, for a diagnosis of AD/HD an individual must present characteristic behaviors across all settings and without a significant amount of aggressive behavior. If the same criteria were adhered to in the United States, the prevalence rates would no doubt be more in line with those of the United Kingdom.[1]

Purpose

To examine prevalence rates of pure AD/HD in a special education sample versus a clinical sample and to consider differences in prevalence if behaviors occurred across settings.

Procedure

Parents and teachers completed the Conners Rating Scales.

Findings

- As hypothesized, the exclusion based on comorbidity reduces prevalence rates for AD/HD.
- Agreement about the occurrence of AD/HD behaviors across settings (teacher and parent) reduces prevalence.
- The behavioral characteristics of subjects vary considerably based on referral source (those in the clinical sample versus those in the special education sample).

Implications

Narrower, more clearly defined criteria are influential in reducing prevalence rates. Comorbid disorders may be overshadowing the AD/HD diagnosis. If the diagnostic parameters remain broad and inclusive, specific intervention strategies will be more difficult to identify. Maybe the incidence of AD/HD has not increased, but rather the number of individuals with comorbid disorders is clouding the issue.

5. Comparison of Diagnostic Criteria for Attention-Deficit Hyperactivity Disorder in a County-wide Sample. Mark L. Wolraich, Jane N. Hannah,

Theodora Y. Pinnock, Anna Baumgaertel, and Janice Brown. (1996).
Journal of American Academy of Child and Adolescent Psychiatry,
35(3), 319–324.

The criteria for AD/HD have been revised with each edition of the *DSM*
(see Appendices A and E). Since the criteria in the *DSM* are used as the
basis for diagnosis of the disorder, it would seem reasonable to expect
changes in prevalence rates with each revision. Mark Wolraich and colleagues set out to test this hypothesis by having teachers rate the same
group of students (8,258 children in grades k–5) using the criteria for *DSM-*
III-R and *DSM-IV*. The teachers completed questionnaires on all of their
students; therefore, the results are based on a non-clinically referred sample
of students contrary to so many of the studies of AD/HD that are done
with clinically referred subjects. *When a study is conducted in a school*
setting with teacher involvement, the findings are so much more relevant
to what we are experiencing in real classrooms everyday.

Results

- There was a 57% increase with *DSM-IV* compared with *DSM-III-R* (possibly
  due to new subtypes).
- There was a higher percentage of girls in AD/HD Inattentive Subtype than in the
  other subtypes (authors suspect girls are underdiagnosed and undertreated because they present fewer externalizing behaviors).
- There was a high incidence of Conduct Disorder (CD)/Oppositional Defiant Disorder (ODD) with AD/HD Hyperactive-Impulsive Subtype (over half).

In conclusion, the new criteria under *DSM-IV* seem to be conducive to
an increase in the identification of AD/HD because it is more sensitive to
previously underdiagnosed subtypes.

6. **Validity of *DSM-IV* ADHD Predominantly Inattentive and Combined**
   Types: Relationship to Previous *DSM* Diagnoses/Subtype Differences.
   Allison E. Morgan, George Hynd, Cynthia A. Riccio, and Josh Hall.
   (1996). *Journal of American Academy of Child and Adolescent Psychi-*
   atry, 35(3), 325–333.

Along with changes in the nomenclature over the years, a greater understanding of the heterogeneity of AD/HD has developed. Researchers are
realizing that there are distinct subtypes of the disorder and that an individual with AD/HD may have characteristics of inattention without having
hyperactivity. Studies indicate that the cognitive, behavioral, and social
manifestations differ between subtypes with inattention and those with hy-

peractivity. These distinctions are reflected in the definition of AD/HD in the fourth edition of the *DSM* (APA, 1994).

The authors of this study refer to the debate over whether the APA acted prematurely in changing the criteria under *DSM-III-R* before there was enough empirical evidence to justify the changes. They set out to compare the diagnostic criteria of *DSM-III* and *DSM-III-R* with that of *DSM-IV* by retrospectively reevaluating subjects (according to *DSM-IV*) who had been diagnosed under one of the previous editions (see Appendices A and E). The participants in this study included clinically referred children who had been evaluated and diagnosed with AD/HD under *DSM-III* or *DSM-III-R*.

Results

Under the new diagnosis according to *DSM-IV* criteria:

- No significant differences were found in diagnosis between subtypes for gender or chronological age.
- Significantly more subjects diagnosed as Predominantly Inattentive Subtype were also diagnosed with a math disability.
- A significantly higher percentage of subjects with AD/HD Combined Type also exhibited characteristics of an externalizing disorder (more aggression, conduct problems, and delinquency were reported by parents and teachers).

The rates of reported incidence may increase under *DSM-IV* compared to *DSM-III* and *DSM-III-R*. *DSM-IV* (APA, 1994) gives more information on the disorder, recognizes the Inattentive Subtype, and results in an increase in prevalence rates.

LABORATORY MEASURES

The three laboratory techniques reviewed in this section are magnetic resonance imaging (MRI), electroencephalogram (EEG), and continuous performance task (CPT). Structural MRI is used to make anatomical images, and functional magnetic resonance imaging (fMRI) is for studying the volume and flow of blood through the brain (Krasuski, Horwitz, & Rumsey, 1996). Both of these techniques provide more information than an X-ray and are less intrusive than other procedures (Krasuski, Horwitz, & Rumsey, 1996). In Study #7, MRI was used since the authors were looking for anatomical brain differences. The future for fMRI is promising as a diagnostic tool in researching brain function (Krasuski, Horwitz, & Rumsey, 1996).

Through the use of EEGs, researchers can study variations in brain wave activity (Tyler & Howard, 1996). The authors of the study included in this section implemented EEG measures in an attempt to differentiate among students with AD/HD, with undifferentiated Attention Deficit Disorder (UADD) and those without AD/HD or UADD.

A characteristic often associated with AD/HD is difficulty sustaining attention to a task (Barkley, 1997; Douglas, 1980; Routh, 1980). One measure that has been used to evaluate an individual's ability to maintain attention is CPT. Penny Corkum and Linda Siegel (1993) reviewed a number of studies on CPT as a diagnostic tool to identify AD/HD. A summary of their article is included in this section.

7. **Prediction of Group Membership in Developmental Dyslexia, Attention Deficit Hyperactivity Disorder, and Normal Controls Using Brain Morphometric Analysis of Magnetic Resonance Imaging.** Margaret Semrud-Clikeman, Stephen R. Hooper, George W. Hynd, Kelly Hern, Rodney Presley, and Tom Watson. (1996). *Archives of Clinical Neuropsychology, 11*(6), 521–528.

The use of MRI as a diagnostic tool for disorders such as AD/HD and Dyslexia is in its infancy. Due to the nonintrusive nature of the procedure, MRI may prove to be a promising additional technique in identifying neurological brain differences in individuals with neuropsychiatric disorders. Until recently, the use of MRI was limited to research purposes. However, studies such as this one are laying the groundwork for the use of MRI as a diagnostic procedure. There needs to be a great deal more research to establish its credibility as a diagnostic tool, but this study is taking us in that direction. Magnetic resonance imaging may some day be used in conjunction with other measures to diagnose AD/HD.

Margaret Semrud-Clikeman and colleagues assigned subjects to one of three groups based on a diagnostic workup including intelligence tests, achievement tests, family histories, and ratings on the *DSM-IV* criteria for AD/HD. The three identified groups were Developmental Dyslexia; Attention Deficit/Hyperactivity Disorder, Combined Type (see Appendix A); and a normal control group. They hypothesized that by using previous research findings regarding brain anomalies they could predict or verify subject membership in the appropriate group.

When using only the results of the MRI the classifications had an accuracy of 60%, and when the I.Q. scores and chronological age were factored in, the accuracy was raised to 87%. No subjects in the clinical groups were misclassified as normal. Based on the results of this study, it appears that MRI may be useful as one component of an AD/HD diagnostic assessment in support of anatomical brain differences in individuals with this disorder. Much research remains to be done to validate these findings before we can even consider moving toward routine MRIs for the identification of AD/HD.

8. **Quantitative EEG Differences in a Nonclinical Sample of Children with ADHD and Undifferentiated ADD.** Samuel Kuperman, Brian Johnson, Stephan Arndt, Scott Lindgren, and Mark Wolraich. (1996). *Journal of American Academy of Child and Adolescent Psychiatry, 35*(8), 1009–1017.

"Undifferentiated Attention Deficit Disorder" was a term used in *DSM-III-R* referring to "Attention Deficit Disorder" without hyperactivity. At the time, there was insufficient evidence to support a category for deficits in attention and cognitive organizational skills (Barkley, 1990). In this context the term UADD is used in reference to AD/HD–Predominantly Inattentive Subtype. This is yet another example of the difficulties in diagnosis presented by a lack of definitive and consistent terminology regarding AD/HD.

In an attempt to more clearly define AD/HD in terms of physiological differences and to establish more definitive diagnostic criteria, EEG procedures were used on nonclinically referred subjects. EEGs provide brain wave recordings. The students were selected from an elementary school district population based on teacher rating scales and assigned to one of three groups: children with AD/HD, children with UADD, and a control group of children without any disruptive behavior disorders. Forty subjects were included in the final study.

Handedness, gender, age, and I.Q. were factored into the analysis to determine if these variables influenced the EEG results. No significant differences were noted between the groups for any of these factors.

Results

The EEG readings suggested

- Subjects in the AD/HD and UADD groups were more alike than either group was to the control group.
- Both attention deficit groups displayed more mental arousal and difficulty judging stimuli than the control group subjects, which affected their ability to sustain attention.
- There was more cerebral activity in subjects with AD/HD (both subtypes) than in control group subjects.

Future research needs to address whether there are distinguishable EEG differences among the three subtypes identified under *DSM-IV*, and between the subtypes and non-AD/HD subjects. Currently, we do not have enough evidence of specific variations on EEG readings to justify its use for diagnosis of AD/HD. EEG use is indicated if seizure disorder is suspected (Baumgaertel, Copeland, & Wolraich, 1996).

9. **Is Continuous Performance Task a Valuable Research Tool for Use with Children with Attention-Deficit-Hyperactivity Disorder?** Penny V. Corkum and Linda S. Siegel. (1993). *Journal of Child Psychology and Psychiatry, 34*(7), 1217–1239.

At first glance, CPT appears to be the answer to the problem of diagnosing AD/HD objectively (in part by removing rater bias). Through the use of a computer monitor and software, an individual's responses to a series of stimuli can be recorded. In this technique, a set of stimuli, usually numerals or letters, are presented to the subject. The student is told what predetermined stimuli to look for and to record a response. The responses are evaluated in terms of the number of errors of omission (targets missed) and commission (selection of nontarget items). Omissions are thought to indicate inattention and commissions to reflect impulsivity.

The study of attention is not as simplistic as this approach implies. Corkum and Siegel examined a number of pertinent studies that used CPT to determine its merits in the diagnostic assessment of AD/HD. They began by looking at the theoretical basis of CPT and whether it actually measured what it was purported to measure.

The reviewers found that in most of the studies reviewed the researchers used CPT to study performance deficits. However, influential variables such as distractions inherent in the test situation, the nature of the task, and performance over time were not considered in any of these studies. The authors therefore concluded that more research is needed to determine the exact nature of AD/HD as demonstrated by task performance analysis before CPT can be considered as a reliable replacement for rating scales. In other words we need to have a better understanding of both the specific deficits at work in AD/HD and how CPT will assess these deficits in an informative way.

Although its popularity among researchers may be premature at this time, the potential for the use of CPT for diagnostic purposes seems to be present. Additional research is needed. *Educators need to keep up with subsequent findings along these lines.* In addition the authors reemphasize the point that the diagnostic criteria for AD/HD need to be more selective for severity and occurrence across settings, as well as to differentiate for comorbidity. This was also suggested in the comparison study (see Study #4, Chapter 4) of *DSM-III-R* and *DSM-IV*.

CHAPTER SUMMARY

Some of the authors in this chapter show us how the definitions and diagnostic criteria have made the identification of AD/HD a very complicated and difficult task. An awareness of this complexity facilitates the understanding of how prevalence rates can vary from one location to another. It is important for us to recognize the characteristic behaviors of children with AD/HD and the risk for negative outcomes to enhance our selection of appropriate interventions. We can leave the official diagnosis to others, but we cannot leave the collaboration with parents and the responsibility of meeting every child's needs to anyone else, nor would we want to do so.

It would behoove us to keep up with the research findings and changes in future editions of the *DSM* as they impact on our effectiveness as educators. The more knowledgeable we are the better we will be able to communicate with parents. This chapter also lays the foundation for Chapter 5, which is a review of research on intervention strategies.

NOTE

1. This study was conducted prior to the publication of *DSM-IV*, which stipulates that the symptoms must be present in at least two settings.

REFERENCES

American Psychiatric Association (APA). (1994). *Diagnostic and statistical manual of mental disorders* (4th ed.). Washington, DC: Author.

Barkley, R. A. (1990). *Attention-Deficit Hyperactivity Disorder: A handbook for diagnosis and treatment*. New York: Guilford Press.

Barkley, R. A. (1997). *ADHD and the nature of self-control*. New York: Guilford Press.

Baumgaertel, A., Copeland, L., & Wolraich, M. (1996). Attention Deficit Hyperactivity Disorder. In M. L. Wolraich (Ed.), *Disorders of development and learning* (pp.424–456). St. Louis, MO: Mosby.

Biederman, J., Faraone, S., Keenan, K., Benjamin, J., Krifcher, B., Moore, C., Sprich-Buckminster, S., Ugaglia, K., Jellinek, M., Steingard, R., Spencer, T., Norman, D., Kolodny, R., Kraus, I., Perrin, J., Keller, M., & Tsuang, M. (1992, September). Further evidence of family-genetic risk factors in Attention Deficit Hyperactivity Disorder. *Archives of General Psychiatry, 49*, 47–57.

Breslau, N., Brown, G., DelDotto, J., Kumar, S., Ezhuthachan, S., Andreski, P., & Hufnagle, K. (1996). Psychiatric sequelae of low-birth-weight at 6 years of age. *Journal of Abnormal Child Psychology, 24*(3), 385–400.

Cohen, M. J., Riccio, C. A., & Gonzalez, J. J. (1994). Methodological differences in the diagnosis of Attention-Deficit Hyperactivity Disorder: Impact on prevalence. *Journal of Emotional and Behavioral Disorders, 2*(1), 31–38.

Corkum, P. V., & Siegel, L. S. (1993). Is continuous performance task a valuable research tool for use with children with Attention-Deficit-Hyperactivity Disorder? *Journal of Child Psychology and Psychiatry, 34*(7), 1217–1239.

Damico, J. S., & Augustine, L. E. (1995). Social considerations in the labeling of students as Attention Deficit Hyperactivity Disordered. *Seminars in Speech and Language, 16*(4), 259–271.

Douglas, V. I. (1980). Treatment and training approaches to hyperactivity: Establishing internal and external control. In C. Whalen & B. Henker (Eds.), *Hyperactive children: The social ecology of identification and treatment* (pp. 283–317). New York: Academic Press.

Dulcan, M. K., & Benson, R. S. (1997). Summary of the practice parameters for the assessment and treatment of children, adolescents, and adults with ADHD. *Journal of American Child Adolescent Psychiatry, 36*(9), 1311–1317.

Faraone, S., Biederman, J., Chen, W., Milberger, S., Warburton, R., & Tsuang, M. (1995). Genetic heterogeneity in Attention-Deficit Hyperactivity Disorder (AD/HD): Gender, psychiatric comobidity, and maternal AD/HD. *Journal of Abnormal Psychology, 102*(2), 334–345.

Faraone, S., Biederman, J., Mennin, D., Gershon, J., & Tsuang, M. (1996). A prospective four-year follow-up study of children at risk for AD/HD: Psychiatric, neuropsychological, and psychosocial outcome. *Journal of American Academy of Child and Adolescent Psychiatry, 35*(11), 1449–1459.

Greene, R. W., Biederman, J., Faraone, S., Ouellette, C., Penn, C., & Griffin, S. M. (1996). Toward a new psychometric definition of social disability in children with Attention-Deficit Hyperactivity Disorder. *Journal of American Academy of Child and Adolescent Psychiatry, 35*(5), 571–578.

Krasuski, J., Horwitz, B., & Rumsey, R. J. (1996). A survey of functional and anatomical neuroimaging techniques. In G. R. Lyon & J. M. Rumsey (Eds.), *Neuroimaging: A window to the neurological foundations of learning and behavior in children* (pp.25–52). Baltimore: Paul H. Brooks.

Kuperman, S., Johnson, B., Arndt, S., Lindgren, S., & Wolraich, M. (1996). Quantitative EEG differences in a nonclinical sample of children with ADHD and undifferentiated ADD. *Journal of American Academy of Child and Adolescent Psychiatry, 35*(8), 1009–1017.

Milberger, S., Biederman, J., Faraone, S., Chen, L., & Jones, J. (1996, September). Is maternal smoking during pregnancy a risk factor for Attention Deficit/Hyperactivity Disorder in children? *American Journal of Psychiatry, 153*(9), 1138–1142

Morgan, A. E., Hynd, G., Riccio, C. A., & Hall, J. (1996). Validity of *DSM-IV* ADHD Predominantly Inattentive and Combined types: Relationship to previous *DSM* diagnoses/subtype differences. *Journal of American Academy of Child and Adolescent Psychiatry, 35*(3), 325–333.

Nemethy, M. (1997, February). Attention Deficit/Hyperactivity Disorder. *Advance for Nurse Practitioners,* 22–29.

Routh, D. K. (1980). Development and social aspects of hyperactivity. In C. Whalen & B. Henker (Eds.), *Hyperactive children: The social ecology of identification and treatment* (pp.55–73). New York: Academic Press.

Semrud-Clikeman, M., Hooper, S. R., Hynd, G. W., Hern, K., Presley, R., & Watson, T. (1996). Prediction of group membership in Developmental Dyslexia, Attention Deficit Hyperactivity Disorder, and normal controls using brain morphometric analysis of magnetic resonance imaging. *Archives of Clinical Neuropsychology, 11*(6), 521–528.

Tyler, R., & Howard, J. (1996). Predicting outcomes for infants and young children by using neuroimaging technology. In G. R. Lyon & J. M. Rumsey (Eds.),

Neuroimaging: A window to the neurological foundations of learning and behavior in children (pp.209–224). Baltimore, MD: Paul H. Brooks.

Wolraich, M. L., Hannah, J. N., Pinnock, T. Y., Baumgaertel, A., & Brown, J. (1996). Comparison of diagnostic criteria for Attention-Deficit Hyperactivity Disorder in a county-wide sample. *Journal of American Academy of Child and Adolescent Psychiatry, 35*(3), 319–324.

5

Studies on Interventions for Attention Deficit/Hyperactivity Disorder

It is not because things are difficult that we do not dare to attempt them, but they are difficult because we do not dare to do so.
—Seneca

The treatment of Attention Deficit/Hyperactivity Disorder (AD/HD) is a process, not a product. There is more involved in how teachers approach meeting the needs of children with AD/HD than just which interventions are used. The effectiveness of a particular technique will vary according to its appropriateness for a particular student (Baumgaertel, Copeland, & Wolraich, 1996). What might work with one person might not work with another. Therefore, a fundamental understanding of the variety of ways in which the disorder may present itself in an individual is crucial to the successful implementation of strategies (Baumgaertel, Copeland, & Wolraich, 1996).

Due to the multifaceted nature of AD/HD, it may be necessary to use multiple treatments (Goldstein & Goldstein, 1990). For example, stimulant medication has been reported to be effective in controlling hyperactivity in many individuals, but long-term academic gains are not unanimously supported by research (Armstrong, 1995; Barkley, 1990; Goldstein, 1997). Research does not support the misconception that medication is the only effective treatment for AD/HD. There seems to be some agreement (even among strong advocates for the use of medication) that this should not be the only intervention used for individuals with AD/HD (Armstrong, 1995; Barkley, 1990, 1997; Phelan, 1993; *Physicians' Desk Reference*, 1995). A combination of procedures across settings may be the most logical approach for such a complex disorder. To treat it with simplicity, believing there is a quick fix, does a disservice to all involved. When considering the efficacy of any strategy, it is important to keep in mind that "One size does not fit all" or even most. It is a misconception that one intervention is equally effective for all students with AD/HD.

Current research on a variety of intervention strategies for use with students with AD/HD and relevant traditional research are reviewed here. Nonmedical techniques are addressed, many are school-based and educationally oriented, including behavior modification, cognitive strategies, academic interventions, and training in social skills. The order of presentation of educational interventions follows the basic development of these techniques historically.

In addition, studies are presented on the use of medication in the treatment of AD/HD, as well as some combined therapies using medication in conjunction with another therapy. Although direct treatment with medication is beyond the scope of educators, it plays a crucial part in the management of many students with the disorder. It is useful for teachers to be aware of the effects of medication and its interaction with other interventions (Phelan, 1993).

EDUCATIONAL INTERVENTIONS

Behavior modification, particularly the use of consequences, is the most commonly practiced classroom intervention for students with AD/HD (Pfiffner & Barkley, 1990). Teachers are familiar with applications of positive reinforcement in the form of praise and tangible rewards (e.g., tokens, stickers), and non-reinforcement or punishment, as in ignoring an undesirable behavior, verbally chastising a student, time-out, and response cost (Pfiffner & Barkley, 1990; Rosén et al., 1984). With all of these techniques, the teacher is administering some consequence to the student with the intention of modifying disruptive or off-task behavior. Although such approaches may affect the target behaviors, there may not be a corresponding improvement in academic performance (Barkley, 1990, 1997; Zentall, 1989). Additionally, because the intervention is externally controlled by the teacher, it is usually effective only within that specific environment and as long as the teacher is using the procedure (Baumgaertel, Copeland, & Wolraich, 1996; Zentall, 1989).

Cognitive-behavioral therapies were developed in an attempt to transfer the responsibility for control to the student with AD/HD based on the premise that self-control was an area of weakness for individuals with the disorder (Abikoff, 1991; Christie, Hiss, & Lozanoff, 1984; Goldstein & Goldstein, 1990; Zentall, 1989). Some approaches included in the cognitive-behavioral category are self-reinforcement, self-monitoring, self-management, and self-talk. These strategies and those mentioned under behavior modification are described as they occur in relation to the research articles reviewed.

Behavior Modification

Contingency management (or use of consequences) may take the form of a token economy in which the student is rewarded for the desired behavior with a token that can later be exchanged for a reward (positive reinforcement). Another contingency system, response cost, involves the loss of a token (punishment) if the appropriate behavior is not displayed by the subject (Bos & Vaughn, 1998; Lewis & Doorlag, 1995; Pfiffner & Barkley, 1990). Time-out is a condition in which an individual is removed from a reinforcing situation to one that is not reinforcing, such as removing a child from the group to sit in the hall or in a quiet chair until he is ready to rejoin the group (Bos & Vaughn, 1998).

The following is an example of the effective use of time-out with a kindergarten student with AD/HD. The child was having difficulty keeping his hands to himself during circle time. The teacher asked him to sit at his desk, which was close to the group. He was allowed to rejoin his classmates after a brief period of time when he was able to control his behavior. The procedure was handled with dignity for the student and resulted in the desired behavior.

Although the use of social praise and ignoring may be effective with non-AD/HD children, those with AD/HD usually require more powerful contingencies to modify behavior and improve academic performance (Barkley, 1990; DuPaul & Stoner, 1994; Solanto, 1990). A study conducted by Robinson, Newby, and Ganzell (1981) using a token system with a group of hyperactive boys in a third-grade classroom showed positive results. All eighteen participants improved in academic performance. The emphasis of this study was on the accurate completion of reading and vocabulary tasks. However, inappropriate disruptive and hyperactive behaviors were reduced because they were incompatible with the targeted behavior (i.e., academic task completion).

Factors affecting the success or failure of contingency approaches are the specific characteristics of the individual for whom it is being designed. It is essential that the rewards be meaningful to the child in order for it to serve as an incentive to change. That is, what might be a reward for one child may not be a reward for another. For this reason teachers should elicit input from the students regarding a reward menu and frequently change the items included (DuPaul & Stoner, 1994; Goldstein & Goldstein, 1990; Pfiffner & Barkley, 1990).

Some students with AD/HD do not respond well to positive reinforcement (Barkley, 1990). *During my years of teaching I have encountered several students who reacted adversely to reward programs. They would actually perform poorly to avoid attention in the form of praise or tangible reinforcements, perhaps because they did not know how to handle it. One particular student would behave inappropriately until he was removed from the class. I quickly discovered that this child worked best by himself, and he did not like being part of a group. The best reinforcement for him was to be allowed to complete his assignments in a private space.* Reinforcers, themselves, may be distracting to children with AD/HD, interfering with their ability to perform the desired behavior (Douglas, 1985).

Lee Rosén and colleagues (1984) conducted four experiments using various combinations of positive and negative consequences with a class of eight hyperactive boys. They found that negative consequences used prudently (delivered consistently and without delay) enhanced the effectiveness of the positive consequences. Negative consequences consisted of time-out (in the hall), verbal reprimands, and loss of free time. The positive consequences were social praise, hugs, and special privileges. Virginia Douglas (1985) pointed out that the balance between negative and positive consequences is crucial. Children with AD/HD tend to become overly impulsive and distracted by rewards. This tendency may be tempered by the clear establishment of rules regarding the loss of a reinforcer (e.g., a token in response cost). However, care should be taken to prevent the frustration that might occur if a student loses more than he earns (Douglas, 1985; Rosén et al., 1984).

In general, research supports the efficacy of contingency management (Barkley, 1990). Mary Solanto (1990) compared the effects of positive reinforcement and punishment (response cost) on impulsivity rates of children with and without AD/HD to see if there was a difference in response between the two groups of subjects. Included in the study were 20 children with AD/HD and 18 normal controls between the ages of 4 1/2 and 11 years. The researcher found that both groups improved equally in performance, under both contingencies (reward and punishment). In other words, there were no differences in performance between groups under either condition.

A combination of reward plus response cost also can be used as an effective means of behavior modification. An example of such an intervention is the use of a marble jar to store marbles that students earn for appropriate behavior and lose for inappropriate behavior. When the jar is full the students receive the promised reward.

In another study, Mark Rapport, Allen Murphy, and Jon Bailey (1982) reported significantly enhanced effects with the use of contingency management (response cost) when compared to the use of stimulant medication (Ritalin) for improving academics and behavior. The authors pointed out that the majority of studies comparing drug therapy to behavior therapy have reported findings in favor of the former. They suggested that contingency-management procedures (as used in this study) may be more powerful than traditional behavior therapy, thus accounting for the different results.

The following reviews are of current studies that focused on the efficacy of specific behavioral interventions for use with students with AD/HD.

1. **Behavioral Treatment of Attention-Deficit Hyperactivity Disorder in the Classroom: The Use of the Attention Training System.** George J. DuPaul, David C. Guevremont, and Russell A. Barkley. (1992). *Behavior Modification, 16*(2), 204–225.

Based on previous research that supported the efficacy of contingency management for use with students with AD/HD (Rapport, Murphy, & Bailey, 1982; Rosén et al., 1984), this study was designed to examine the effects of response cost and directed rehearsal on academic performance and classroom behavior. The subjects were two boys with AD/HD, ages 6 and 7 years, who were in a self-contained special education class. The response-cost intervention was implemented through the use of the Attention Training System (ATS) (Gordon Systems, Inc., 1987), a battery operated device that provided positive and negative feedback to the subject. The teacher monitored student off-task behavior and used a remote control to signal the child when he was off-task. The ATS included a module, which was placed on the student's desk, that tallied and displayed the number of points earned. At the appropriate time the child could trade points for various rewards.

The directed-rehearsal procedure consisted of instruction or modeling of the academic activity by the teacher or aide, followed by additional seatwork for the student. This technique was used if the subject failed to earn a designated number of points for on-task behavior during specific phases of the experiment.

Both students showed significant improvement over baselines in attending and completing classwork under the response-cost (ATS) condition. According to the researchers, the findings were unclear as to whether or not the addition of the directed-rehearsal contingency was an enhancement over the ATS alone.

The teacher and the aide preferred the use of the ATS to the use of tokens due to the ease of monitoring student behavior. They chose to continue using the program after the experiment was completed. The students also expressed an interest in the continued use of this approach.

2. **Promoting Academic Performance in Inattentive Children: The Relative Efficacy of School-home Notes with and without Response Cost.** Mary Lou Kelley and Alyson P. McCain. (1995). *Behavior Modification, 19*(3) 357–375.

Because AD/HD behaviors occur across settings (e.g., school and home) successful interventions are most effective when they are coordinated between teachers and parents. In this study response cost was used at home in conjunction with daily notes from educators reporting to parents on their children's behavior for the day. The authors cited a number of other studies supporting the efficacy of parent-managed contingencies as compared to teacher-managed programs for improving academic performance (Ayllon, Garber, & Pisor, 1975; Budd et al., 1981; Karraker, 1972).

Typically, a daily report card provides spaces to record the students' academic and classroom behavior. For example, attending to task, remaining seated, completing classwork, and being prepared for class, as well as a space for homework assignments, may be included (DuPaul & Stoner, 1994).

Five children with AD/HD, between the ages of 6 and 9 years, were selected as subjects. The teachers evaluated the students' classroom behavior each day and the parents administered consequences based on the daily report. The study was designed to assess the effectiveness of school-home notes, both with and without response cost, to increase the students' on-task behavior and completion of assignments. An initial baseline was established and two interventions were randomly assigned during the treatment phase (one with response cost and one without). Procedures, behaviors, and rewards or contingencies were clearly established by parents, teachers, and students before the experiment began.

Subjects improved in academic performance and classroom behavior with the use of school-home notes, especially when response cost was also implemented. The teachers stated that this form of intervention (school-home notes) was not only beneficial to the students, but it did not require any changes in routine or demands on their time.

One of the greatest complaints of teachers is that there is never enough time to accomplish all that they need to in a day. The approach outlined in this article was not only effective with the five students involved, but it was manageable within the time constraints of the educators. However, as a fellow educator pointed out to me, one challenging aspect of this approach is ensuring that parents will follow up on their part of the agreement.

Parents should be involved in planning the interventions and should have an understanding of reinforcement procedures prior to implementation to ensure success (DuPaul & Stoner, 1994). *An example of the importance of parent training is depicted in the following scenario. As part of a technology grant, all fifth graders in a particular elementary school were given home computers with Internet access to use for homework and research. Many parents, seeing how excited their children were using this technology, began withholding computer privileges as punishment for misbehavior. Al-*

though computer usage was a salient reward, using it as a punishment defeated the purpose of the grant.

3. Effects of Reward and Response Cost on the Performance and Motivation of Children with ADHD. Caryn L. Carlson, Miranda Gaub, and David K. Alexander. (In press). *Cognitive Therapy and Research*.

Definition of Terms

contingencies: punishment or reward for the occurrence of a specific behavior (Goldenson, 1984)

reinforcer: a stimulus (as a reward or the removal of discomfort) that is effective esp. in operant conditioning because it regularly follows a desired response (*Merriam-Webster's*, 1987, p.993)

response cost: removal of reinforcer when the undesired behavior occurs (e.g., token loss) (Bos & Vaughn, 1998)

Caryn Carlson, Miranda Gaub, and David Alexander cited earlier research on how the use of contingencies (punishment or reward) affected the learning and behavior of children with AD/HD. For example, Douglas (1985) found that the use of rewards could have negative effects on the performance of children with this disorder if the students became distracted by the reinforcers (e.g., tokens) or frustrated by failing to earn the reward. Other studies have shown positive results with the use of negative consequences (e.g., response cost) (Kelley & McCain, 1995; Rapport, Murphy, & Bailey, 1982; Solanto, 1990). However, the authors of this study noted that there was inconsistent support in the research regarding children with AD/HD having a positive response to punishment. In some cases performance actually suffered. They felt this inconsistency in the research warranted further study comparing the effects of punishment and reward on children with AD/HD. As a result, they decided to examine the different effects of reward and response cost (punishment) on performance and motivation in children with and without AD/HD.

The participants included in the study were 40 children with AD/HD and 40 control children without AD/HD, ages 8 to 12 years. There were 27 boys and 13 girls in each group. The children were asked to complete an arithmetic task under one of three conditions (response cost, reward, or no contingency). In the reward condition, tokens were given for correctly completed items. In the response-cost condition, tokens were given beforehand and taken away for incorrect or incomplete items. No tokens were used in the no-contingency setting.

Across all three conditions, subjects with AD/HD had fewer problems correct and completed fewer problems than control subjects. In other words, the AD/HD subjects had a poorer performance than non-AD/HD subjects regardless of the intervention. A comparison of test scores for just the students with AD/HD, across the three conditions, indicated that response cost resulted in more problems correct than with reward or no contingency.

In an attempt to assess motivation, participants were given a free-choice task to complete. The children were allowed to select either another set of math problems or a set of spelling exercises to do. Subjects were also asked to rate themselves on motivation. The results indicated:

- Neither response cost nor reward had a negative effect on self-perceptions of performance or motivation.
- Students with AD/HD in the response-cost condition were more motivated during the free-choice task than students with AD/HD in either of the other conditions.

In summary, according to the findings of this study, response cost was more effective than reward in improving the performance and motivation of children with AD/HD.

4. **Methylphenidate and Attentional Training.** Mark D. Rapport, Sandra Loo, Patti Isaacs, Susan Goya, Colin Denney, and Sean Scanlan. (1996). *Behavior Modification, 20*(4), 429–450.

Of the numerous therapies suggested in the treatment of AD/HD, stimulant medication and behavioral interventions have received the most support and study among researchers (Barkley, 1990; Rapport, 1992). Prior to this study, the authors reported, no study had been conducted that looked at the effectiveness of both psychostimulants (e.g., Ritalin, Dexedrine, Cylert) and behavioral training for girls with AD/HD. Therefore, the focus of this study was to examine the response of female subjects with AD/HD to stimulant medication (i.e., Ritalin) and attentional training techniques. In this experiment, an electronic device, the ATS (Gordon Systems, Inc., 1987), was used to record the child's attention while completing a computer task. Points were awarded for on-task behavior and deducted for off-task behavior. At the end of the session, points could be traded for tangible rewards (e.g., stickers, gum). The device was activated by the experimenter who was observing the subject. The ATS was also used in a study conducted by DuPaul, Guevremont, and Barkley (1992) (see Study #1 in this chapter).

The subjects in this study were two six-year-old fraternal twin girls who met the criteria for AD/HD and Oppositional Defiant Disorder (ODD) according to the *DSM-III-R* (APA, 1987) (see Appendix E). Both subjects responded positively to the two treatments. These positive results were similar to those reported for boys treated with stimulant medication and behavioral interventions (Pelham et al., 1989), suggesting that the effectiveness of the combined treatments may not be affected by gender. It was recommended to the parents that a combined approach be used for optimal results with their daughters. The authors stated that previous trials on stimulant medication alone had not been as effective with these twin girls.

Cognitive-behavioral Therapy

In part, cognitive-behavioral therapies were developed based on the premise that some individuals needed direct instruction on skills (Schumaker & Sheldon, 1985) rather than learning intuitively by observing and imitating the behavior of others (Bandura, 1969). According to Albert Bandura's theory of social learning, children learn behaviors, as well as values, through exposure to the models around them. An example of copied behavior is an infant waving "bye-bye" as someone leaves. This type of incidental learning is often an area of weakness for children with AD/HD (Barkley, 1997; Meichenbaum, 1977). Instead, the action must be specifically modeled with explicit directions (Copeland & Love, 1995; Meichenbaum, 1977; Schumaker & Sheldon, 1985). By using direct instruction along with the modeling of self-talk, it was hypothesized that individuals with AD/HD would be able to develop the self-control necessary for successful learning that most people develop intuitively (Bandura, 1969; Barkley, 1990; Goldstein & Goldstein, 1990; Keogh & Barkett, 1980; Schumaker & Sheldon, 1985).

Lev Vygotsky (1962) proposed a three-stage theory of language acquisition that fostered the development of cognitive-behavioral therapies. The first stage is external speech, which is the expression of thoughts in words. Children begin this process by saying words and then sentences in an attempt to control their environment and to communicate. Egocentric speech is the second stage and it consists of speaking aloud to oneself. When engaging in egocentric speech the child does not need an audience and in fact is often oblivious to the response or presence of others.

Whereas external speech is social and interactive, egocentric speech is more like thinking out loud and is functionally the same as the third stage, which is inner speech (Vygotsky, 1962). Egocentric speech, "the link between overt and inner speech . . . readily assumes a planning function, i.e., turns into thought proper quite naturally and easily" (p.45). In other words, Vygotsky believed that egocentric speech served in the transition of speech from external to inner. Through the use of external tools or signs the student is able to solve internal problems. A cognitive example of this process is when children use mnemonics or counting on their fingers to solve problems, and then make the transition to counting and problem solving in their heads.

Inner speech represents the merging of thought and language and brings with it self-regulation. Behavior of a young child is regulated externally through commands from adults and stimuli from the environment. The development of inner speech enables the child to plan and reflect before acting (Diaz, Neal, & Amaya-Williams, 1990). Self-regulation is a process involving the regulation of attention, memory, concentration, and problem solving through the use of a plan of action that the individual has formulated (Diaz, Neal, & Amaya-Williams, 1990). This cognitive process is also referred to as executive function (Castellanos, 1997). Executive *dysfunction*, that is, the inability to self-regulate impulsivity, attention, concentration, memory, and problem-solving strategies, is characteristic of individuals with AD/HD (Castellanos, 1997).

If the natural progression of language, as described by Vygotsky, proceeds from external to internal (Goldstein & Goldstein, 1990; Goldstein, 1997), some children with AD/HD may have a deficit due to an inability to transfer, without assistance, from external to internal control through self-talk (Barkley, 1997; Goldstein & Goldstein, 1990; Goldstein, 1997; Meichenbaum, 1997).

A study was conducted by Meichenbaum (1977) of the egocentric speech of 16 four-year-olds in their preschool setting. Half of the children were impulsive, and the other half were considered reflective. The amount of egocentric talk did not differ significantly in amount between the two groups, but the quality varied in essential ways. The impulsive subjects engaged in more self-stimulating private speech (e.g., chanting, animal noises, nonsense words); whereas, the reflective children used self-regulatory speech and adjusted their self-talk to meet the demands of the task at hand. In conclusion, Meichenbaum believed the results suggested that impulsive children used inner speech with less maturity and regard for the specific nature of the situation than reflective preschoolers. These findings are supported by the work of Kohlberg, Yaeger, and Hjertholm (1968); Piaget (1955); Maccoby, Dowley, Hogan, and Degerman (1965); Meichenbaum and Goodman (1976); and Zentall (1989).

Typically, cognitive-behavioral therapies include strategies that are designed to enhance self-control through self-regulatory processes (Barkley, 1997; DuPaul & Stoner, 1994; Meichenbaum, 1977; Zentall, 1989). Self-regulation includes actions taken by an individual for the purpose of altering one's own behavior and consequently the outcome (Barkley, 1997). Methods of accomplishing this change in outcome usually involve self-directed activities beginning with having the individual observe his or her own behavior (DuPaul & Stoner, 1994; Zentall, 1989). It is essential to recognize the inappropriate behavior before attempting to change it (Copeland & Love, 1995; Meichenbaum, 1977; Zentall, 1989).

Self-monitoring can be used to identify and record maladaptive behaviors when they occur. Usually, an external cue is implemented initially, as in behavior modification, possibly in the form of a signal from the teacher or an electronic device such as a tape player. However, in cognitive-behavioral modification, the external cue is faded out after the subject has internalized the ability to self-monitor (DuPaul & Stoner, 1994; Meichenbaum, 1977; Zentall, 1989). Through the paired use of cuing and modeling, the responsibility for changing behavior is transferred from an external source (e.g., teacher, parent, device) to the internal mechanisms of the student (Christie, Hiss, & Lozanoff, 1984; Meichenbaum, 1977; Zentall, 1989).

Self-monitoring can play a crucial part in this process by helping the individual develop the ability to recognize the inappropriate behavior, as well as the frequency of its occurrence. By identifying the undesired behaviors, the teacher may begin to employ strategies to improve the subject's repertoire of reactions (Meichenbaum, 1977). Self-talk (verbalization of actions and thought) should be modeled and then rehearsed in order for most individuals with AD/HD to successfully develop mature use of inner speech (Barkley, 1997; Meichenbaum, 1977).

Christie, Hiss, and Lozanoff (1984) conducted a study on the use of self-monitoring procedures, along with teacher cuing, to modify the behavior of a group of hyperactive children. The researchers intentionally selected a regular classroom setting to avoid the difficulty in transferring training procedures from the laboratory setting to the classroom, which has been noted as one of the drawbacks in the use of cognitive-behavioral therapies (Barkley, 1990, 1997; Christie, Hiss, & Lozanoff, 1984). According to Russell Barkley (1997), "The most useful treatments will be those that are in place in natural settings at the point of performance where the desired behavior is to occur" (p.338). The results of the study by Christie, Hiss, and Lozanoff (1984) support this contention.

The students involved in the experiment were trained to record and classify their off-task and inattentive behavior as depicted on a previously videotaped recording. After training, the teacher observed and recorded the student's behavior and signaled the student to do so as well. The findings indicated that this method of self-recording with teacher signaling led to an increase in on-task and appropriate behavior. Another benefit of self-monitoring is that it can actually cause a change in behavior as a result of the process itself (Heins, Lloyd, & Hallahan, 1986; Reid & Harris, 1993). In other words, the undesirable behavior may become modified without the need for further intervention.

The two main focuses of self-monitoring within educational research have been time-on-task (amount of time the student continues working on the task) and cognitive behavior (actual time the student spends solving the problem or completing the task) (Goldstein & Goldstein, 1990; Reid & Harris, 1993). An example of time-on-task might be the amount of time a student remains seated at a desk working on a math worksheet rather than engaging in off-task behaviors such as getting a drink of water, sharpening a pencil, or staring out the window. How well the student completed the math problems on the worksheet reflects cognitive behavior. Time-on-task is measured by quantity of time, as compared to cognitive behavior, which is measured by quality of task performance.

Some researchers contend that as a result of more time and attention devoted to the task, academic performance will improve (Heins, Lloyd, & Hallahan, 1986; McDougall & Brady, 1998), whereas others argue that an increase in awareness of cognitive behaviors will result in greater time-on-task (Reid & Harris, 1993).

Robert Reid and Karen Harris (1993) conducted a study comparing the differential effects of self-monitoring of attention and self-monitoring of academic performance with a group of 28 students with learning disabilities. The authors suggested that both forms of intervention increased on-task behavior, but self-monitoring for performance yielded greater gains in accuracy and skill maintenance over time. However, the authors noted, "There does not appear to be a 'best' method of self-monitoring for all students on all tasks" (p.29). As previously mentioned, the specific characteristics of the individual influence the effectiveness of the intervention. *Although the subjects of this study were identified as learning disabled, due to the high comorbidity of learning disabilities with AD/HD (Biederman, Newcorn, & Sprich, 1991), the findings may have relevance to educators.*

The focus of the following two articles was attention-to-task and academic performance.

5. **Initiating and Fading Self-management Interventions to Increase Math Fluency in General Education Classes.** Dennis McDougall and Michael P. Brady. (1998). *Exceptional Children, 64*(2), 151–166.

Typically, self-management techniques have been studied in special education settings involving only disabled students (Kern et al., 1994). Such procedures are used to increase the amount of time students spend on their academic tasks, which is referred to as time-on-task (Christie, Hiss, & Lozanoff, 1984). In contrast, this study took place in a general education classroom, and the subjects were a combination of students with and without disabilities. The purpose of this research was to compare the effectiveness and generalization of skills with two different self-monitoring approaches. One software program focused on time-on-task and the other focused on increased academic performance (in math).

There were five fourth-grade students who participated. Three were full-time regular education students, one was an AD/HD student in the regular classroom receiving only consultant special education services, and one was a learning disabled (LD) student who spent most of the day in the general education class with some time in the resource room. The method of implementation was self-directed by each student. The students self-monitored, self-recorded and graphed progress, self-cued (with audiotape), self-assessed, and self-rewarded.

Participants earned tokens based on improvement over their own base-line scores, not through competing with peers. Gradually, the experimenters faded out the self-management system. When audio-cuing equipment was removed, the students were directed to ask themselves if they were on task. When recording forms were phased out, the students recorded directly on their math worksheets. Modifications had to be made for the student with AD/HD because she was not improving quickly enough. Changes were made in the frequency and statement used for cuing with this student, due to her problems with inattention and distractibility.

Results

- Percentage of correct math problems increased for all participants during the intervention and was maintained throughout fading for all but the AD/HD student.
- Engaged time increased for all five participants, even during the fading time.
- Engaged time was slightly higher when the students were monitoring academic performance than when they were monitoring attention to task.
- Generalization of math fluency improved for all participants except the one with AD/HD. For her it remained stable.

Although the student with AD/HD improved in math fluency and engaged time, her gains were not maintained during the fading-out phase, nor did the skills generalize. As noted, modifications were made for this student to enhance her rate of improvement. The authors suggested that researchers explore additional adaptations to self-monitoring methods that might be more effective for students with AD/HD, as well as combining its uses with other techniques.[1]

6. **Attentional Focus of Students with Hyperactivity during a Word-search Task.** Sydney S. Zentall, Arlene M. Hall, and David L. Lee. (In press). *Journal of Abnormal Psychology.*

The issue of self-control, or a lack thereof, has been associated with AD/HD (Barkley, 1997). In the classroom setting, self-control plays an important part in the student's ability to work with others and to complete assignments independently (Zentall, Hall, & Lee, in press). The authors of this article referred to several methods that have been used to enhance self-control in children, including self-monitoring. Because most self-monitoring techniques have limitations in that they typically require adult supervision and feedback for initial implementation, these researchers wanted to examine a method of self-monitoring that overcame these limitations. The use of a mirror was selected as a means of directing the students' attention to themselves as a way of improving performance.

Forty-three middle-school students were selected to participate in the study. There were 16 students in the *more active* and *inattentive* group (8 boys and 8 girls). The comparison group consisted of 27 students (15 boys and 12 girls) characterized as *less active* and *more attentive* than the treatment group. The participants were selected on the basis of teacher nominations. Teachers completed rating scales for all students included in the study.

The children were asked to complete a partially solvable word search under two different conditions. In one situation there was a mirror mounted on the wall directly in front of the student. The other condition was identical to the first, but there was a blank wall, instead of a mirror, in front of the student. The experimenters examined student performance on the task under the two different conditions for both groups of subjects.

It was hypothesized that through the use of a mirror, self-control would increase and performance would improve. Performance improvement was measured by the word-search task. The results showed that students in the high-activity, low-attention group performed better in the mirrored condition, especially if they looked in the mirror (as compared to just being influenced by its presence). Students in the comparison group actually showed a performance loss in the mirrored condition. Sydney Zentall, Arlene Hall, and David Lee (in press) explained the improvement in the target group in terms of increased self-focus and self-control. In other words, the external cue (i.e., the mirror) served as a signal to the student to exercise self-control.

7. **Computer-assisted Cognitive Training for ADHD.** Dilnavaz B. Kotwal, William J. Burns, and Doil D. Montgomery. (1996). *Behavior Modification, 20*(1), 85–96.

This was a case study. The subject was a thirteen-year-old boy in the sixth grade who had been diagnosed with AD/HD. He was experiencing behavior problems at home and disruptive behavior and problems with inattention at school. Special services were provided through the LD department in English, math, and spelling.

The purpose of the study was to evaluate the use of computer-assisted cognitive training for an individual with AD/HD. The intervention consisted of 35 sessions over a three-month period on a computerized system that was developed to improve such cognitive skills as attention, concentration, memory, problem-solving, and reasoning. These cognitive skills are classified under executive function as it is defined in the introduction to the chapter, and the cognitive training involved the development of the subject's self-regulation of these skills. The software package used was Captain's Log by Sanford and Browne (1988). Another program cited in this article was THINKable from IBM (Psychological Corporation/Harcourt Brace Jovanovich, 1991).

Results

The student:

- improved in all areas measured on the Conners Parent Rating Scale.
- showed a gradual decrease in impulsive-hyperactive behavior in weekly scores on the abbreviated Conners Parent Rating Scale.
- improved on some subtests, but showed a decline in behavior on others as measured by the Conners Teacher Rating Scale.
- maintained most gains, but at a slightly lower level, at the seven-month follow-up evaluation.
- improved in academic grades from Ds and Fs to Bs and Cs.
- improved in time-on-task and was less disruptive in class, according to teacher reports.
- was successfully mainstreamed for most classes.

Kotwal, Burns, and Montgomery pointed out that the positive results of this case study lend support to the value in using computer software for cognitive training for children with AD/HD. Due to the increased access to computers in classrooms, this treatment should be fairly easy to administer.

Academic Interventions

Academic interventions consist of modifications in methods of instruction, instructional materials, or the classroom environment (DuPaul & Eckert, 1997). Examples of modifications in instruction might include the teacher's use of direct instruction, cooperative learning teams (Fowler, 1994), or peer tutoring (Kohler & Strain, 1990). Materials can be enhanced for students with AD/HD through an adjustment in the length of the assignment, the addition of color cues or the element of novelty, and by providing structure to the task (Fowler, 1994).

Modifications to the classroom environment may take the form of the physical placement of a student's desk near the teacher or the establishment of organizational procedures and structured lessons (Fowler, 1994). *An example of a relatively simple intervention is allowing the student with AD/HD to select two seats within the classroom to be used at his discretion throughout the school day. This technique worked effectively with a child who had been unresponsive to medication, several behavioral modification programs, and professional counseling.*

Although there are many sources of suggestions for academic modifications for use in the classroom, there is a dearth of empirical data regarding the effectiveness of such techniques (Burcham, Carlson, & Milich, 1993; Fiore, Becker, & Nero, 1993; Greenwood, Carta, & Hall, 1988). The reader is referred to Appendix I for a list of *Guidelines for Educational Interventions* (Fowler, 1994; see also Appendix J).

A number of studies on academic interventions, specifically targeting students with AD/HD, have been conducted by Zentall and colleagues (Zentall, 1989, 1993; Zentall, Falkenberg, & Smith, 1985; Zentall & Meyer, 1987), dealing with modifications in instructional techniques and materials, and classroom environment. Studies reviewed also include the work of DuPaul and Henningson (1993), Greenwood, Carta, and Hall (1988), and Kohler and Strain (1990) focusing on peer tutoring.

The studies selected for review in this section are intended to give teachers an indication of the research that is being conducted and some of the findings. The list is not intended to be all inclusive or conclusive, but rather to add to the reader's ever-growing knowledge base regarding academic interventions for use with students with AD/HD. As I have mentioned previously, the purpose of this book is to enhance mindful decision making on the part of educators so that they can better meet the needs of their students.

8. Structured Tasks: Effects on Activity and Performance of Hyperactive and Comparison Children. Sydney S. Zentall and Susan L. Leib. (1985). *Journal of Educational Research, 79*(2), 91–95.

The work of William Cruickshank (1975) and Alfred Strauss and Laura Lehtinen (1947) laid the groundwork for the study of the benefits of structure for students with attentional deficits and hyperactivity. The purpose of Sydney Zentall and Susan Leib's study was to evaluate the effect of task structure on the academic performance of students with and without hyperactivity. Hyperactivity was regarded as excessive activity that results in disruptive or off-task behaviors, thus inhibiting the student's ability to attend. The authors stated that an art lesson was selected in order to provide an activity that the hyperactive subjects would be able to perform as well as the nonhyperactive subjects. By selecting such an activity, they believed they could minimize the effects of the differing ability levels among the students. Individuals with AD/HD were seen as more likely to have academic deficits.

The subjects included 15 boys with hyperactivity and 16 boys without hyperactivity between the ages of 9 and 13 years in grades 3 through 6. Eight boys from each type (with and without hyperactivity) were randomly assigned to the group that would first participate in a highly structured task and then in a task with low structure. The remaining subjects were assigned to a second group that began with a low-structure task and proceeded to a highly structured task. Within the high-structure activity students were directed to copy or reproduce designs of two models using precut paper squares. In the low-structure task students were to create original designs with the same number of paper squares.

There was significantly more activity in the low-structure condition for all subjects (those with and without hyperactivity). The authors concluded that added structure to a task decreased student activity level. *The implication for educators is that by adding structure to a lesson it may be possible to reduce the activity and the associated distracting behaviors of students with hyperactivity.*

9. **Effects of Color Stimulation and Information on the Copying Performance of Attention-Problem Adolescents.** Sydney S. Zentall, Steven D. Falkenberg, and Linda B. Smith. (1985). *Journal of Abnormal Child Psychology, 13*(4), 501–511.

As emphasis shifted away from the idea that children with AD/HD were oversensitive to stimulation, the thought emerged that students with the disorder were actually seeking to maintain high levels of stimulation (Douglas, 1980). Instead of thriving in a distraction-free environment, it was believed that such students would seek out stimulation (Barkley, 1990). Thus, the optimal stimulation theory was developed by psychologists, who stated that the hyperactive student seeks high levels of stimulation and becomes disengaged or easily bored with repetitive tasks (Zentall, Falkenberg, & Smith, 1985).

Based on the optimal stimulation theory, it was hypothesized that performance could be enhanced through the use of increased visual stimulation (Zentall, Falkenberg, & Smith, 1985). The researchers conducted this study to determine if the addition of color cues to a writing task would improve copying skills in adolescents with attention problems. Specifically, color was added to difficult letter parts and randomly to other letters.

It has been suggested that individuals with AD/HD may not have a problem with over- or underarousal; instead, they have difficulty adjusting the level of arousal to match the demands of the task (Douglas, 1980). In this study color was used to highlight salient information for successful letter formation in an attempt to help the students adjust their level of attention to meet the task requirements (i.e., handwriting).

As a learning disabilities specialist, I would often mark important parts of letters, words, or numbers to facilitate student learning. In this way, attention was drawn to the essential aspects of the task that my students may not have recognized.

Thirty-two junior and senior high-school boys were selected for the study. One-half were rated as being highly active with attention problems and poor handwriting. The remaining 16 were normal controls without hyperactivity or attentional deficits, but they did have poor handwriting. As had been predicted, the handwriting performance of the adolescents with attention problems improved with the color-coding technique, but no improvement was noted in the performance of the subjects in the control group. The authors noted that the use of stimulation was effective when used with repetitive copying tasks (i.e., handwriting). The following study addresses the use of attentional cuing for more complex tasks (i.e., spelling) (Zentall, 1989).

10. **Attentional Cuing in Spelling Tasks for Hyperactive and Comparison Regular Classroom Children.** Sydney S. Zentall. (1989). *Journal of Special Education, 23*(1), 83–93.

The present study was designed as an extension of previous research using color cuing to increase sustained attention and improve the task performance of hyperactive children (Zentall, Falkenberg, & Smith, 1985). Whereas stimulation has been used to enhance attention to salient details, researchers have found that stimulation can also act as a distraction that interferes with task performance if attention is drawn to nonrelevant details (Rosenthal & Allen, 1980; Zentall, Zentall, & Barack, 1978; Zentall, Zentall, & Booth, 1978). In other words, individuals with AD/HD tend to seek stimulation regardless of whether it is associated with essential or nonessential details. The indiscriminate use of color cuing may actually do more harm than good if it serves as a distraction from the learning task. In this context, a visual stimulus was used to draw a student's attention to a specific task (Zentall, 1989).

The purpose of this study was to define what constituted the effective use of novel stimuli to enhance task performance (i.e., spelling). For the experiment, 20 hyperactive and 26 nonhyperactive boys in grades three through six were presented with spelling tasks with and without color coding. The order of task presentation was varied between black letters first, then letters with color added, and the reverse order of trials.

The investigators found that the hyperactive boys outperformed the control group when color was added during practice rather than in the beginning when initial learning was taking place. A spelling task was used because it required selective attention as compared to a simpler task such as handwriting. The implication for educators is to use nondistracting stimuli (e.g., black letters) during the introduction of new, difficult skills, and add color during the rote-practice phase of learning with hyperactive children.

11. **Peer Tutoring Effects on the Classroom Performance of Children with Attention Deficit/Hyperactivity Disorder.** George J. DuPaul and Patri-

cia North Henningson. (1993). *School Psychology Review*, 22(1), 134–143.

Students with AD/HD benefit from direct instruction, immediate feedback, and individualized instruction (Pfiffner & Barkley, 1990). Teachers, however, have too many students and not enough time to meet the additional demands of students with this disorder (Kohler & Strain, 1990). Peer tutoring can be used to alleviate the pressure on a teacher to personally meet the individual needs of each student (DuPaul & Stoner, 1994; Kohler & Strain, 1990).

Additionally, by using active response procedures, the excess energy of some AD/HD students that might otherwise result in disruptive behavior can be redirected (Zentall & Meyer, 1987). Peer tutors may provide the extra help needed to implement such procedures (DuPaul & Stoner, 1994). For a review of peer-mediated methods, the reader is referred to *The Use of Peer Tutoring Strategies in Classroom Management and Educational Instruction* (Greenwood, Carta, & Hall, 1988).

DuPaul and Henningson presented a case study of the effects of a class-wide peer-tutoring program on a student with AD/HD. The intervention was designed based on a program developed by Greenwood, Delquadri, and Carta (1988). The subject was a seven-year-old male in second grade who had been diagnosed with AD/HD. He was experiencing academic difficulties, particularly in mathematics. After a baseline was established for the target student, peer tutoring in mathematics was implemented.

Results

- There was an increase in the subject's on-task behavior with peer tutoring.
- The subject's math performance improved.
- The subject's attention to instruction more than doubled in frequency over the baseline.

The authors attributed the effectiveness of peer tutoring to the methods of instruction used. The one-on-one instruction was geared to the ability level and instructional pace of the student with AD/HD, as compared to a traditional, didactic approach more typically used with whole-class instruction. Through the use of peer tutoring, the aforementioned modifications were put in place that were conducive to student learning. The implication is that through changes in method of delivery, the needs of all students can be met and peer tutoring can be used to facilitate those instructional adjustments (DuPaul & Henningson, 1993).

A colleague shared a story with me of a mismatch between instructional methods being used and the individual needs of a boy with AD/HD. A group of middle-school teachers requested the assistance of an educational consultant to help them deal with this student. My friend spent a full day observing the target subject in his various classes. It was apparent that the young man was not only AD/HD, but also rather intelligent, perhaps even gifted. However, he was experiencing academic as well as behavioral problems at school.

At the beginning of each class, the student appeared interested and anxious to participate, but he quickly lost interest when his attempts to interact were ignored. In all but one class, the teachers lectured and allowed only limited student involvement. Even the consultant became restless and bored with this method of instruction.

One teacher used an alternative approach in which the students worked in cooperative groups. In this class, all of the students thrived and the student with AD/HD was indistinguishable from his classmates.

This entire scenario depicts the need to use good teaching practices to enhance learning for all students, especially those with AD/HD. Even if a teacher feels limited by large class size, there are alternative ways of individualizing instruction and making lessons interactive. Peer tutoring and cooperative teams are two examples.

School-based Interventions

12. The Effects of School-based Interventions for Attention Deficit Hyperactivity Disorder: A Meta-analysis. George J. DuPaul and Tanya L. Eckert. (1997). *School Psychology Review*, 26(1), 5–27.

Definition of Terms

academic intervention: an intervention that focuses primarily on manipulating academic instruction or academic materials (DuPaul & Eckert, 1997, p.8)

cognitive-behavioral intervention: an intervention that focuses on the development of self-control skills and reflective problem-solving strategies (DuPaul & Eckert, 1997, p.8)

contingency-management intervention: teacher-mediated reinforcement or punishment to establish or reduce target behaviors (DuPaul & Eckert, 1997, p.8)

meta-analysis: an analysis of a number of studies that focus on the same question and use similar variables (Ary, Jacobs, & Razavieh, 1996)

A meta-analysis was conducted on 63 studies of the effectiveness of interventions. All of the studies:

• were school based,

• had AD/HD subjects,

- had no subjects on medication,
- were conducted between 1971 and 1995.

The types of interventions included were:

- academic (e.g., modification of structure, peer tutoring, use of instructional manipulatives),
- contingency-management (e.g., reward, response cost, punishment),
- cognitive-behavioral (e.g., self-talk, cognitive rehearsal, self-instruction, self-reinforcement).

Results

The meta-analysis showed:

- an increase in the number of studies of school-based interventions over the 24 years.
- that most of the studies were of contingency-management and cognitive-behavioral interventions.
- that most of the participants were from public schools and placed in general education classes for at least part of the day.
- that there were significant behavioral effects of school-based interventions, regardless of the techniques used.
- that there was greater improvement in classroom behavior as the result of contingency-management and academic interventions, than due to cognitive-behavioral interventions.
- that there was greater enhancement of academic performance by cognitive-behavioral interventions than by contingency-management or academic interventions.

This may be interpreted by teachers as an indication that the type of intervention selected should be based on the desired change within a school setting. If one is seeking to improve classroom behavior, contingency-management and academic interventions seem to be more effective than cognitive-behavioral interventions. However, academic performance seems to be influenced more by cognitive-behavioral interventions than by contingency-management and academic interventions.

13. Who Are the Children with Attention Deficit-Hyperactivity Disorder? A School-Based Survey. Robert Reid, John W. Maag, Stanley F. Vasa, and Gregg Wright. (1994). *Journal of Special Education, 28*(2), 117–137.

Most researchers of AD/HD focus on children who are referred to a clinic; those who study AD/HD in schools usually look at students in special education placements (Barkley, 1990). The authors examined a school-based sample of students who were medically diagnosed with AD/HD. The purpose was to get an accurate description of how children with AD/HD are served within a school setting, with attention paid to special education services provided (types and range), modifications and interventions implemented, and student achievement.

Findings

Demographic information:

- The number of students identified with AD/HD increased in grades one through six and reached a peak at third grade.
- The distribution of AD/HD by ethnic group was similar to the proportion of each group within the general school-district population (with the exception of Hispanics). No Hispanics were identified with AD/HD even though they made up 2.4% of the district population.

Disability categories:

- Fifty-seven percent of the students identified with AD/HD were receiving special education services.
- Over half of the AD/HD students receiving special education services were labeled Behaviorally Disordered (BD).
- The next largest category with AD/HD was LD (28.6%).
- Five percent of the students identified with AD/HD also qualified for the Mental Retardation category.
- Students with AD/HD, particularly in the LD or BD categories, were more likely to also qualify for speech and language services (7.8%).
- Only one student with AD/HD was labeled Other Health Impaired (OHI). (When this study was done in 1994, this was a new category for AD/HD.)

Placement:

- The majority of students identified with AD/HD were served in regular education classrooms. Additional services were provided on a resource level for students who qualified for special education.
- Only a small percentage (8%) were served totally outside of the regular classroom.

Academic achievement:

- Even though some students with AD/HD experience academic difficulties, findings *from this study* did not support the notion of AD/HD as a basis for underachievement. The academic performance of students with AD/HD was commensurate with that of students without AD/HD as measured by standardized math and reading tests.

Educational treatment:

- In this study, over 90% of the students identified with AD/HD were on medication.
- In over 50% of the cases where medication was prescribed there was no physician contact with the school.
- Students with AD/HD receiving special education services had more interventions and accommodations than AD/HD students not receiving special education services.
- The majority of AD/HD students were served in general education classrooms.

If the general education classroom is where the *majority* of AD/HD students spend the *majority* of their time, then "a very real need exists to provide general education classroom teachers with both knowledge of ADHD and a repertoire of techniques to deal with the problems students with ADHD may experience in the general classroom environment" (Reid, Maag, Vasa, & Wright, 1994, p.133).

There also needs to be more communication between teachers and physicians if medication is going to remain a major intervention treatment for AD/HD (Turecki, 1997). Teachers are often asked to monitor medication, but they feel ill equipped to do so, especially if there is a lack of guidance from the health-care provider.

Social Skills Training

Most children with AD/HD experience difficulty getting along with parents, peers, siblings and teachers (Frederick & Olmi, 1994). Upon entering the school setting, the student with AD/HD is faced with a new set of demands to behave and interact appropriately with others (Barkley, 1990). High levels of activity and impulsivity that were tolerable in a less-structured setting may become areas of concern for educators (Frederick & Olmi, 1994).

By first grade, parents of AD/HD children often are confronted with complaints from teachers regarding the child's inappropriate and immature social behaviors, as well as emerging academic difficulties (Barkley, 1990). Thus, the introduction of the classroom environment and all of the problems inherent in homework may exacerbate an already difficult situation. As the AD/HD behaviors begin to spill over into a number of settings, parents and educators may need to work together to develop techniques that are effective across situations (Barkley, 1990; Frederick & Olmi, 1994).

The following study is an evaluation of the effectiveness of a social skills training program involving parents. Although the training was not conducted in the classroom, the transfer of social skills to the educational setting was assessed through teacher ratings.

14. **Parent-assisted Transfer of Children's Social Skills Training: Effects on Children with and without Attention-Deficit Hyperactivity Disorder.** Fred Frankel, Robert Myatt, Dennis P. Cantwell, and David T. Feinberg. (1997, August). *Journal of American Academy of Child and Adolescent Psychiatry, 36*(8), 1056–1064.

Peer rejection has been seen by researchers as part of the clinical profile of many individuals with AD/HD (Frankel, Myatt, Cantwell, & Feinberg, 1997). Theoretically, by improving social skills, peer rejection would decrease. Although interventions typically do not generalize across settings (e.g., home and school) for children with AD/HD, especially those comorbid with ODD (see Appendix D for APA definition), it was hypothesized that by involving parents as a component of the social skills training program there would be generalization of those skills by the children from school to home.

The treatment group was comprised of 35 children with AD/HD, 14 children without AD/HD, and 19 children with ODD. Two subjects with ODD were in the non-AD/HD group. Twenty-four children (one-half with AD/HD and one-half without AD/HD) were in a control group that received no treatment. Within the control group, five were diagnosed with ODD. All subjects with AD/HD were on medication. The treatment consisted of 12 sessions of social skills training for the children and concurrent sessions for parents.

The AD/HD subjects who received social skills training showed comparable gains in social skills to those without AD/HD, according to both parent and teacher ratings. Likewise, subjects with ODD who received social skills training had gains comparable to those without ODD. Children in the treatment group had outcomes better than the majority (83%) of the subjects not receiving treatment. The improvement in social skills was measured by parent and teacher rating scales.[2]

MEDICAL INTERVENTIONS

Since 1937, stimulant medication (i.e., Ritalin, Dexedrine, and Cylert) has been the primary treatment for AD/HD (Swanson et al., 1991; Zametkin & Rapoport, 1987). It has been well established in the research that psychostimulants have a positive effect on behavior, but the evidence is not yet available for long-term academic gains (Arnold et al., 1997; Nemethy, 1997; Swanson et al., 1991).

Statistics on stimulant medication indicate that its use for the treatment of AD/HD has doubled every four to seven years since 1971. Twenty-five percent of the students in special education programs are on stimulant medication. There has been an increase in medical treatment for girls, students on the secondary level, and children with inattention without hyperactivity (Wilens & Biederman, 1992).

The issue of dosing effect is an important consideration in the use of medication for AD/HD. At higher doses of stimulant medication, hyperactivity decreases and social behaviors improve, but cognitive performance declines (Goldstein, 1997; Nemethy, 1997; Wilens & Biederman, 1992). It is therefore recommended that lower doses over briefer periods of time may be more effective than increased dosages (Shaywitz et al., 1982; Turecki, 1997). This is contrary to the belief that "if some is good more must be better" (Turecki, 1997).

Although studies (Barkley, 1990, 1997; Goldstein & Goldstein, 1990; Turecki, 1997; Wilens & Biederman, 1992) show that approximately 70% of children with AD/HD respond to stimulant medication, there is a sizable minority that does not. The reason for this lack of response in some children remains elusive. Comorbidity may be a factor. Poorer responses to stimulant medication have been noted in AD/HD children who suffer from anxiety or depression (Wilens & Biederman, 1992). There are other drugs that may be prescribed for individuals who do not respond to the stimulants. A survey of their efficacy in the treatment of AD/HD and potential side effects goes beyond the scope of this book (see Appendix H, Medications Used in the Treatment of AD/HD). For more comprehensive coverage of medical interventions, refer to *Attention, Please* by Edna D. Copeland and Valerie L. Love (1995).

A great deal of research has been conducted over the years on the use of stimulant medication for the treatment of AD/HD (Turecki, 1997). Two studies were selected for review. Christopher Gillberg and colleagues (1997) dealt with a long-term treatment using stimulant medication. Josephine Elia and colleagues (1993) compare two psychostimulant medications. These studies were selected because they deal with the efficacy of stimulant medication either in terms of length of time or type of medication.

15. **Long-term Stimulant Treatment of Children with Attention-Deficit Hyperactivity Disorder Symptoms.** Christopher Gillberg, Hans Melander, Anne-Liis von Knorring, Lars-Olof Janols, Gunilla Thernlund, Bruno Hagglof, Lena Eidevall-Wallin, Peik Gustafsson, and Svenny Kopp. (1997, September). *Archives of General Psychiatry, 54,* 857–864.

Definition of Term

placebo: a neutral substance given to subjects in an experiment to make them believe they are receiving a treatment (Ary, Jacobs, & Razavieh, 1996, p.572)

For sixty years, stimulant medication has been used to control hyperactivity, inattention, and distractibility in children (Zametkin & Rapoport, 1987). According to Gillberg and colleagues (1997), most researchers have focused on short-term effects of stimulant medication. Gillberg et al. wanted to examine the long-term effect of pharmacological interventions on behavior and cognition. The treatment consisted of the use of stimulant medication versus a placebo for children with symptoms of AD/HD over a fifteen-month period.

Sixty-two children with AD/HD were included in the study. There were 52 boys and 10 girls between the ages of 6 and 11 years. All subjects had to have an I.Q. above 50. Participants were given the Wechsler Intelligence Scale for Children–Revised (WISC-R) as an assessment of general intelligence. The Conners Teacher Rating Scale and the Conners Parent Rating Scale were completed on each child in the study. All assessments were completed periodically throughout the experiment.

Results

- The medication-treatment group showed gains on the WISC-R and a reduction in AD/HD behaviors, over the placebo group.
- The medication-treatment group had a slower and later dropout rate (from the study) than the placebo group.

According to the findings of this study, long-term treatment with stimulant medication yielded positive effects in both cognitive and behavioral domains.

16. **Classroom Academic Performance: Improvement with Both Methylphenidate and Dextroamphetamine in ADHD Boys.** Josephine Elia, Patricia A. Welsh, Charles S. Gullotta, and Judith L. Rapoport. (1993). *Journal of Child Psychology and Psychiatry, 34*(5), 785–804.

Definition of Terms

dextroamphetamine: (d-amphetamine) a stimulant medication—brand name Dexedrine (Anastopoulous, DuPaul, & Barkley, 1991)

double-blind experiment: an experimental technique in which neither the observers nor the subjects know who is receiving the experimental treatment (Ary, Jacobs, & Razavieh, 1996)

methylphenidate: a stimulant medication—brand name Ritalin (Anastopoulous, DuPaul, & Barkley, 1991)

placebo: a neutral substance given to subjects in an experiment to make them believe they are receiving a treatment (Ary, Jacobs, & Razavieh, 1996, p.572)

Academic difficulties and school failure are associated with AD/HD (Barkley, 1990; Goldstein & Goldstein, 1990). There is evidence of short-term improvement in academic performance with the use of stimulant medication (Armstrong, 1995). However, according to Elia et al. (1993), the majority of studies on the effects of stimulant medication on academic achievement used methylphenidate (Ritalin). The authors wanted to examine the efficacy of methylphenidate compared to dextroamphetamine (Dexedrine) for the development of math and reading skills.

A double-blind experiment was designed. Neither the observers nor the subjects knew who was taking dextroamphetamine (Dexedrine), methylphenidate (Ritalin), or a placebo. Thirty-three male students (ages 6–12) at a day hospital school participated in an eleven-week study. The first two weeks were used to establish a baseline on each participant before medicine was administered. The boys were assessed on math and reading skills.

Findings

- Students on either stimulant medication attempted more math and reading tasks than students taking the placebo.
- Students on either medication got a greater percentage correct on reading tasks than students in the placebo group.
- The students on dextroamphetamine (Dexedrine) improved in the percentage correct on math tasks.
- Similar side effects occurred in subjects taking either drug, including decreased appetite, difficulty sleeping, meticulous behavior, and increased feelings of sadness.

In conclusion, these results indicate short-term improvement in academic performance with the two stimulant medications when compared to the placebo.

CHAPTER SUMMARY

The complexity of AD/HD is reflected in the research on interventions. Regardless of the type of strategy examined, the success was dependent, at least in part, on the specific circumstances. Even with stimulant medication, the oldest and most used treatment for the disorder, other factors had to be considered. While the short-term efficacy of psychostimulants to control behavior are supported by research, other techniques have proven more effective in the enhancement of academic skills (Rapport, Murphy, & Bailey, 1982).

Although all of the school-based interventions studied had positive results, specific outcomes depended upon strategy selection. This was apparent in the improved classroom behavior with the use of contingency management versus improved academic performance when cognitive-behavioral approaches were implemented (see Study #12). In Study #6, students with AD/HD improved in a word-search task if a mirror was present, but students without AD/HD actually had a decline in skills in the mirrored condition. This illustrates the necessity to be aware of the factors that impact upon an intervention's effectiveness under specific conditions.

There is no one intervention that will be the answer to all of the challenges presented by AD/HD. It is crucial that teachers remain focused on the child and not the disorder. Through capitalizing on a student's strengths and recognizing specific weaknesses, modifications can be designed and implemented to meet individual needs.

Recently, I had the occasion to visit a second grade classroom. The teacher shared her frustrations with me regarding a student she identified as having many AD/HD characteristics. The boy's parents refused to have him tested by school personnel or evaluated by a physician for a medical diagnosis. The prevailing belief in this particular school was that medication was the only solution to this child's difficulties. The challenging behaviors that I observed were inattention, lack of organization, and failure to complete assignments. The student did not display any disruptive behaviors while I was present.

When the teacher consulted the principal, she was told that the only thing she could do was to let the child fail second grade, then the parents would realize they had to put him on medication. What a frightening thought that some educators feel compelled to punish a child out of a sense of limited options.

There were a number of strategies that the teacher could have used with this student that did not require a medical diagnosis of AD/HD. By helping the child succeed, the school could have built a better relationship with the parents, not to mention the impact of success on the child. This approach would have been better than trying to force the parents to have their child put on medication, because there is a sizable minority (25–30%) (Barkley, 1990, 1997; Goldstein & Goldstein, 1990; Turecki, 1997; Wilens & Biederman, 1992) of individuals who do not respond to stimulant medication. Teachers are responsible for meeting their educational needs as well.

The interventions reviewed in this chapter are not intended to be exhaustive. Rather, teachers should view this information as a basis for developing meaningful approaches to use in their classrooms. Table 5.1 is a summary of the findings and implications of the studies included in this chapter. It is provided to give educators a feel for the limitless possibilities waiting to be developed to meet the unique challenges presented by individuals with AD/HD.

Table 5.1
Summary of Results on Studies on Interventions

Type of Intervention	Findings	Educational Implications
Educational Interventions		
Behavior Modification		
1. Response cost with Attention Training System	• Improvement in attending and completing classwork	• Findings support use of response costs and ATS for AD/HD in the classroom
Subjects: 2 males with AD/HD		
2. School-home notes and response cost	• Improved academic performance and classroom behavior with school-home notes, especially in conjunction with response cost	• Effective intervention with relative ease of administration • Parental involvement is a crucial factor
Subjects: 5 students with AD/HD		
3. Reward and response cost	• More positive results for AD/HD subjects with response cost than reward, on performance and motivation	• Findings support the use of response cost over reward, in the classroom, for students with AD/HD
Subjects: 40 children with and 40 without AD/HD		
4. Methylphenidate and attentional training	• Subjects responded to the combination of two therapies after an unsuccessful trial of medication alone	• Educators can enhance the effects of medication through the implementation of other interventions
Subjects: a set of twin girls		
Cognitive-behavioral Therapy		
5. Self-management (with computer)	• Improved academic performance (short term) • Increased time-on-task • Generalization for all but AD/HD student	• Findings indicate need for additional modifications and interventions for AD/HD students
Subjects: 5 fourth-grade students, 1 with AD/HD		
6. Attentional focus (through the use of a mirror)	• Performance improved on a word-search task under mirrored condition	• Findings suggest students with AD/HD may have improved self-control by redirecting focus to self (e.g., with mirrors)
Subjects: 43 middle-school students		

Table 5.1 (*continued*)

Type of Intervention	Findings	Educational Implications
7. Computer-assisted cognitive training A case study	• Improved behavior, grades, time-on-task	• Findings support value of Captain's Log in classroom for students with AD/HD
Academic Interventions		
8. Structured tasks Subjects: 15 boys with and 16 boys without hyperactivity	• Highly structured tasks resulted in lower levels of activity for both groups of subjects	• Educators may be able to reduce activity levels and associated distracting behaviors of students with hyperactivity through increased task structure
9. Color stimulation Subjects: 16 high school boys with and 16 without AD/HD	• Improved copying skills with the use of color coding for subjects with AD/HD	• Teachers may enhance repetitive task (e.g., handwriting) performance for AD/HD students through the use of color-coding techniques
10. Attentional cuing Subjects: 20 boys with and 26 without hyperactivity	• Hyperactive boys outperformed controls when color coding was used during practice of a spelling task • Color coding may be distracting to AD/HD students if it is used during initial learning of complex skills	• Findings suggest educators use nondistracting stimuli during introduction of difficult skills and color cuing during rote practice for hyperactive students
11. Peer tutoring A case study	• Increased on-task behavior • Improved math performance • Increased attention to instruction	• Findings suggest peer tutoring may be an effective classroom strategy for meeting the special needs of students with AD/HD

Table 5.1 (*continued*)

Type of Intervention	Findings	Educational Implications
School-based Interventions		
12. Meta-analysis	• Significant behavioral effects with all school-based interventions • Improved classroom behavior with academic procedures and contingency management • Improved academic performance with cognitive-behavioral interventions	• To improve classroom behavior, use contingency-management and academic strategies • To improve academic performance use cognitive-behavioral interventions • Intervention selection is situation or student specific
13. Survey	• 90% of students with AD/HD were on medication • The majority of AD/HD students were served in regular education classrooms • AD/HD students served in the regular classroom had fewer interventions and modifications	• Based on this survey, it seems that more interventions for AD/HD students are needed in regular education classrooms
Social Skills Training		
14. Parent-assisted social skills training	• All subjects who received treatment had outcomes better than 83% of those not receiving treatment	• The findings supported the use of parent training and assistance as a component of a social skills program for students with AD/HD, to enhance generalization to the classroom
Subjects: treatment group of 35 subjects with AD/HD, 14 without AD/HD, and a control group of 24 subjects, 1/2 with and 1/2 without AD/HD		
Medical Interventions		
15. Long-term stimulant treatment	• Subjects in the medication treatment group improved cognitively and behaviorally	• Findings support the efficacy of long-term stimulant medication treatment in cognitive and behavioral domains
Subjects: 52 boys with AD/HD and 10 girls with AD/HD		

93

Table 5.1 (*continued*)

Type of Intervention	Findings	Educational Implications
16. Methylphenidate and dextro-amphetamine Subjects: 33 boys with AD/HD	• Both stimulants enhanced reading performance • The number of math problems attempted increased on both medications • Math performance improved with dextroamphetamine	• Educators should see academic improvements with students treated with either of these medications

Note: Chart numbers correspond with article review numbers.

There are more possibilities in nature, in the elements, in man and out of man; and they come as fast as man sees and knows how to use these forces, in nature and in himself. Possibilities and miracles mean the same thing.

—Prentice Mulford

NOTES

1. For additional information on self-management techniques see Appendix F, Self-management Techniques Resource List.

2. For more information on social skills training refer to Appendix G, Social Skills Resource List.

REFERENCES

Abikoff, H. (1991). Cognitive training in AD/HD children: Less to it than meets the eye. *Journal of Learning Disabilities, 24*(4), 205–209.

American Psychiatric Association (APA). (1987). *Diagnostic and statistical manual of mental disorders* (3rd ed., revised). Washington, DC: Author.

Anastopoulos, A. D., DuPaul, G. J., & Barkley, R. A. (1991). Stimulant medication and parent training therapies for Attention Deficit-Hyperactivity Disorder. *Journal of Learning Disabilities, 24*(4), 210–218.

Armstrong, T. (1995). *The myth of the A.D.D. child.* New York: Dutton.

Arnold, L. E., Abikoff, H. B., Cantwell, D. P., Conners, C. K., Elliot, G., Greenhill, L. L., Hechtman, L., Hinshaw, S. P., Hoza, B., Jensen, P. S., Kraemer, H. C., March, J. S., Newcorn, J. H., Pelham, W. E., Richters, J. E., Schiller, E., Severe, J. B., Swanson, J. M., Vereen, D., & Wells, K. (1997, September). National Institute of Mental Health collaborative multimodal treatment study of children with ADHD (the MTA). *Archives of General Psychiatry, 54*, 865–870.

Ary, D., Jacobs, L., & Razavieh, A. (1996). *Introduction to research in education.* Orlando: Holt, Rinehart, & Winston.

Ayllon, T., Garber, S., & Pisor, K. (1975). The elimination of discipline problems through a combined school-home motivational system. *Behavior Therapy, 6*, 616–626.

Bandura, A. (1969). *Principles of behavior modification.* New York: Holt, Rinehart, & Winston.

Barkley, R. A. (1990). *Attention-Deficit Hyperactivity Disorder: A handbook for diagnosis and treatment.* New York: Guilford Press.

Barkley, R. A. (1997). *ADHD and the nature of self-control.* New York: Guilford Press.

Baumgaertel, A., Copeland, L., & Wolraich, M. (1996). Attention Deficit Hyperactivity Disorder. In M. L. Wolraich (Ed.), *Disorders of development and learning* (pp.424–456). St. Louis, MO: Mosby.

Biederman, J., Newcorn, J., & Sprich, S. (1991). Comorbidity of Attention Deficit Hyperactivity Disorder with Conduct, Depressive, Anxiety, and other disorders. *American Journal of Psychiatry, 148*(5), 564–577.

Bos, C. S., & Vaughn, S. (1998). *Strategies for teaching students with learning and behavior problems.* Needham Heights, MA: Allyn and Bacon.

Budd, K. S., Leibowitz, J. M., Riner, L. S., Mindell, C., & Goldfarb, A. L. (1981). Home-based treatment for severe disruptive behaviors: A reinforcement package for preschool and kindergarten children. *Behavior Modification, 5*(2), 273–298.

Burcham, B., Carlson, L., & Milich, R. (1993). Promising school-based practices for students with Attention Deficit Disorder. *Exceptional Children, 60*(2), 174–180.

Carlson, C. L., Gaub, M., & Alexander, D. K. (In press). Effects of reward and response cost on the performance and motivation of children with ADHD. *Cognitive Therapy and Research.*

Castellanos, F. X. (1997). Approaching a scientific understanding of what happens in the brain in AD/HD. *Attention, 4*(1), 30–35.

Christie, D. J., Hiss, M., & Lozanoff, B. (1984). Modification of inattentive classroom behavior: Hyperactive children's use of self-recording with teacher guidance. *Behavior Modification, 8*(3), 391–406.

Copeland, E. D., & Love, V. L. (1995). *Attention, please: ADHD/ADD.* Plantation, FL: Specialty Press.

Cruickshank, W. M. (1975). The learning environment. In W. Cruickshank & D. Hallahan (Eds.), *Perceptual and learning disabilities in children* (pp.227–277). Syracuse, NY: Syracuse University Press.

Diaz, R. M., Neal, C. J., & Amaya-Williams, M. (1990). The social origins of self-regulation. In L. C. Moll (Ed.), *Vygotsky and Education: Instructional implications and applications of sociohistorical psychology* (pp.127–154). Cambridge: Cambridge University Press.

Douglas, V. I. (1980). Treatment and training approaches to hyperactivity: Establishing internal and external control. In C. Whalen & B. Henker (Eds.), *Hyperactive children: The social ecology of identification and treatment* (pp.283–317). New York: Academic Press.

Douglas, V. I. (1985). The response of ADD children to reinforcement. In L. M. Bloomingdale (Ed.), *Attention Deficit Disorder: Identification, course, and treatment rationale* (pp.49–65). New York: Spectrum Publications.

DuPaul, G. J., & Eckert, T. L. (1997). The effects of school-based interventions for

Attention Deficit Hyperactivity Disorder: A meta-analysis. *School Psychology Review, 26*(1), 5–27.

DuPaul, G. J., Guevremont, D. C., & Barkley, R. A. (1992). Behavioral treatment of Attention-Deficit Hyperactivity Disorder in the classroom: The use of the Attention Training System. *Behavior Modification, 16*(2), 204–225.

DuPaul, G. J., & Henningson, P. N. (1993). Peer tutoring effects on the classroom performance of children with Attention Deficit/Hyperactivity Disorder. *School Psychology Review, 22*(1), 134–143.

DuPaul, G. J., & Stoner, G. (1994). *AD/HD in the schools: Assessment and intervention strategies.* New York: Guilford Press.

Elia, J., Welsh, P. A., Gullotta, C. S., & Rapoport, J. L. (1993). Classroom academic performance: Improvement with both methylphenidate and dextroamphetamine in ADHD boys. *Journal of Child Psychology and Psychiatry, 34*(5), 785–804.

Fiore, T. A., Becker, E. A., & Nero, R. C. (1993). Educational interventions for students with Attention Deficit Disorder. *Exceptional Children, 60*(2), 163–173.

Fowler, M. (1994, October). *Briefing paper: Attention-Deficit/Hyperactivity Disorder.* Washington, DC: National Information Center for Children and Youth with Disabilities (NICHCY).

Frankel, F., Myatt, R., Cantwell, D. P., & Feinberg, D. T. (1997, August). Parent-assisted transfer of children's social skills training: Effects on children with and without Attention-Deficit Hyperactivity Disorder. *Journal of American Academy of Child and Adolescent Psychiatry, 36*(8), 1056–1064.

Frederick, B. P., & Olmi, D. J. (1994). Children with Attention Deficit/Hyperactivity Disorder: A review of the literature on social skills deficits. *Psychology in the Schools, 31*, 288–296.

Gillberg, C., Melander, H., von Knorring, A., Janols, L., Thernlund, G., Hagglof, B., Eidevall-Wallin, L., Gustafsson, P., & Kopp, S. (1997, September). Long-term stimulant treatment of children with Attention-Deficit Hyperactivity Disorder symptoms. *Archives of General Psychiatry, 54*, 857–864.

Goldenson, M. (Ed.). (1984). *Longman dictionary of psychology and psychiatry.* New York: Longman.

Goldstein, S. (1997). *Managing learning and attention disorders in late adolescence and adulthood.* New York: Wiley.

Goldstein, S., & Goldstein, M. (1990). *Managing attention disorders in children.* New York: Wiley.

Gordon Systems, Inc. (1987). The attention training system. Dewitt, NJ: Author.

Greenwood, C. R., Carta, J. J., & Hall, R. V. (1988). The use of peer tutoring strategies in classroom management and educational instruction. *School Psychology Review, 17*(2), 258–275.

Greenwood, C. R., Delquadri, J., & Carta, J. J. (1988). *Classwide peer tutoring.* Seattle, WA: Educational Achievement Systems.

Heins, E. D., Lloyd, J. W., & Hallahan, D. P. (1986). Cued and noncued self-recording of attention to task. *Behavior Modification, 10*(2), 235–254.

Karraker, R. J. (1972). Increasing performance through home-managed contingency programs. *Journal of School Psychology, 10*(2), 173–179.

Kelley, M. L., & McCain, A. P. (1995). Promoting academic performance in inattentive children: The relative efficacy of school-home notes with and without response cost. *Behavior Modification, 19*(3), 357–375.

Keogh, B. K., & Barkett, C. J. (1980). An educational analysis of hyperactive children's achievement problems. In C. Whalen & B. Henker (Eds.), *Hyperactive children: The social ecology of identification and treatment* (pp.259–282). New York: Academic Press.

Kern, L., Dunlap, G., Childs, K. E., & Clark, S. (1994). Use of a classwide self-monitoring program to improve the behavior of students with emotional and behavioral disorders. *Education and Treatment of Children, 17*(3), 445–458.

Kohlberg, L., Yaeger, J., & Hjertholm, E. (1968). Four studies and a review of theories. *Child Development, 39*, 691–736.

Kohler, F. W., & Strain, P. S. (1990). Peer-assisted interventions: Early promises, notable achievements, and future aspirations. *Clinical Psychology Review, 10*, 441–452.

Kotwal, D. B., Burns, W. J., & Montgomery, D. D. (1996). Computer-assisted cognitive training for ADHD. *Behavior Modification, 20*(1), 85–96.

Lewis, R. B., & Doorlag, D. H. (1995). *Teaching special students in the mainstream.* Englewood Cliffs, NJ: Prentice-Hall.

Maccoby, E., Dowley, E., Hogan, J., & Degerman, R. (1965). Activity level and intellectual functioning in normal school children. *Child Development, 36*(3), 761–770.

McDougal, D., & Brady, M. P. (1998). Initiating and fading self-management interventions to increase math fluency in general education classes. *Exceptional Children, 64*(2), 151–166.

Meichenbaum, D. (1977). *Cognitive-behavior modification: An integrative approach.* New York: Plenum Press.

Meichenbaum, D., & Goodman, S. (1976). Critical questions and methodological problems in studying private speech. In G. Zivin (Ed.), *Development of self-regulation through speech.* New York: Wiley.

Merriam-Webster's collegiate dictionary (9th ed.). (1987). Springfield, MA: Merriam-Webster.

Nemethy, M. (1997, February). Attention Deficit/Hyperactivity Disorder. *Advance for Nurse Practitioners*, 22–29.

Pelham, W. E., Walker, J. L., Sturges, J., & Hoza, J. (1989). Comparative effects of methylphenidate on ADD girls and ADD boys. *Journal of the American Academy of Child and Adolescent Psychiatry, 28*(5), 773–776.

Pfiffner, L. J., & Barkley, R. A. (1990). Educational placement and classroom management. In R. A. Barkley (Ed.), *Attention Deficit Hyperactivity Disorder: A handbook for diagnosis and treatment* (pp.498–539). New York: Guilford Press.

Phelan, T. (1993). *All about Attention Deficit Disorder.* Glen Ellyn, IL: Child Management, Inc.

Physicians' desk reference (49th ed.). (1995). Montvale, NJ: Medical Economics Data Production Company.

Piaget, J. (1955). *The language and thought of the child.* New York: New American Library.

Psychological Corporation/Harcourt Brace Jovanovich. (1991). THINKable Rehabilitation System [Computer program]. San Antonio, TX: Author (555 Academic Court, San Antonio, TX 78204).

Rapport, M. D. (1992). Treating children with Attention-Deficit Hyperactivity Disorder. *Behavior Modification, 16*(2), 155–163.

Rapport, M. D., Loo, S., Isaacs, P., Goya, S., Denney, C., & Scanlan, S. (1996). Methylphenidate and attentional training. *Behavior Modification, 20*(4), 429–450.

Rapport, M. D., Murphy, H. A., & Bailey, J. S. (1982). Ritalin vs. response-cost in the control of hyperactive children: A within-subject comparison. *Journal of Applied Behavior Analysis, 15*(2), 205–216.

Reid, R., & Harris, K. R. (1993). Self-monitoring of attention versus self-monitoring of performance: Effects on attention and academic performance. *Exceptional Children, 60*(1), 29–40.

Reid, R., Maag, J. W., Vasa, S. F., & Wright, G. (1994). Who are the children with Attention Deficit-Hyperactivity Disorder? A school-based survey. *Journal of Special Education, 28*(2), 117–137.

Robinson, P. W., Newby, T. J., & Ganzell, S. L. (1981). A token system for a class of underachieving hyperactive children. *Journal of Applied Behavioral Analysis, 14*(3), 307–315.

Rosén, L. A., O'Leary, S. G., Joyce, S. A., Conway, G., & Pfiffner, L. J. (1984). The importance of prudent negative consequences for maintaining the appropriate behavior of hyperactive students. *Journal of Abnormal Child Psychology, 12*(4), 581–604.

Rosenthal, R. H., & Allen, T. W. (1980). Intra-task distractibility in hyperactive and nonhyperactive children. *Journal of Abnormal Child Psychology, 8*(2), 175–187.

Sanford, J. A., & Browne, R. J. (1988). Captain's Log [Computer software]. Richmond, VA: Braintrain.

Schumaker, J. B., & Sheldon, J. (1985). *Learning strategies curriculum: The sentence writing strategy.* Lawrence: University of Kansas.

Shaywitz, S. E., Hunt, R. D., Jatlow, P., Cohen, D. J., Young, J. G., Pierce, R. N., Anderson, G. M., & Shaywitz, B. A. (1982). Psychopharmacology of Attention Deficit Disorder: Pharmacokinetic, neuroendocrine, and behavioral measures following acute and chronic treatment with methylphenidate. *Pediatrics, 69,* 688–694.

Solanto, M. V. (1990). The effects of reinforcement and response cost on a delayed response task in children with Attention Deficit/Hyperactivity Disorder: A research note. *Child Psychology and Psychiatry, 31*(5), 803–808.

Strauss, A. A., & Lehtinen, L. E. (1947). *Psychopathology and education of the brain-injured child.* New York: Grune and Stratton.

Swanson, J. M., Cantwell, D., Lerner, M., McBurnett, K., & Hanna, G. (1991). Effects of stimulant medication on children with ADHD. *Journal of Learning Disabilities, 24*(4), 219–230.

Turecki, S. (1997, November). *Practical psychopharmacology for children.* Paper presented at the meeting of the Nurse Practitioner Associates for Continuing Education (NPACE), Boston, MA.

Vygotsky, L. S. (1962). *Thought and language* (E. Hanfmann & G. Vaker, Eds. and Trans.). Cambridge, MA: MIT Press.

Wilens, T. E., & Biederman, J. (1992). The stimulants. *Psychiatric Clinics of North America, 15*(1), 87–118.

Zametkin, A. J., & Rapoport, J. L. (1987). Neurobiology of Attention Deficit Disorder with hyperactivity: Where have we come in 50 years? *American Academy of Child and Adolescent Psychiatry, 26*(5), 676–686.

Zentall, S. S. (1989). Attentional cuing in spelling tasks for hyperactive and comparison regular classroom children. *Journal of Special Education, 23*(1), 83–93.

Zentall, S. S. (1993). Research on the educational implications of Attention Deficit/Hyperactivity Disorder. *Exceptional Children, 60*(2), 143–153.

Zentall, S. S., Falkenberg, S. D., & Smith, L. B. (1985). Effects of color stimulation and information on the copying performance of attention-problem adolescents. *Journal of Abnormal Child Psychology, 13*(4), 501–511.

Zentall, S. S., Hall, A. M., & Lee, D. L. (In press). Attentional focus of students with hyperactivity during a word-search task. *Journal of Abnormal Psychology*.

Zentall, S. S., & Leib, S. L. (1985). Structured tasks: Effects on activity and performance of hyperactive and comparison children. *Journal of Educational Research, 79*(2), 91–95.

Zentall, S. S., & Meyer, M. J. (1987). Self-regulation of stimulation for ADD-H children during reading and vigilance task performance. *Journal of Abnormal Child Psychology, 15*(4), 519–536.

Zentall, S. S., Zentall, T. R., & Barack, R. S. (1978). Distractions as a function of within-task stimulation for hyperactive and normal children. *Journal of Learning Disabilities, 11*(9), 540–548.

Zentall, S. S., Zentall, T. R., & Booth, M. E. (1978). Within-task stimulation: Effects on activity and spelling performance in hyperactive and normal children. *Journal of Educational Research, 71*(4), 223–230.

6

Tying It All Together

Knowledge has three degrees—opinion, science, illumination.
—Plotinus

Based upon a review of the literature and current research, three predominant themes emerge concerning working with individuals with Attention Deficit/Hyperactivity Disorder (AD/HD): the need to provide classroom teachers with the skills and knowledge to select appropriate interventions, the need for factual information to dispel misconceptions, and the need for collaboration among all those concerned with the education of the AD/HD child. The first theme, which is the purpose of this book and has been addressed throughout, is to empower teachers by providing them with knowledge about AD/HD so that they can select and implement appropriate strategies to enhance the learning of students with AD/HD. This type of decision making can happen only when there is an understanding of the disorder in all its complexity. Through increased knowledge, greater collaboration, and enhanced ability to select appropriate interventions we can increase the likelihood that students with AD/HD will experience greater success in school.

The remaining two themes, regarding misconceptions and collaboration, are the focus of this chapter. Pertinent research is reviewed and collaborative roles are identified.

MISCONCEPTIONS

A review of the research was conducted in an attempt to develop a knowledge base to enhance meaningful decision making. Five commonly held misconceptions on AD/HD have been identified that are refuted by the research. The misconceptions coincide with specific chapters.

Misconception #1

AD/HD behaviors are caused by poor parenting, a lack of discipline, and junk-food diets (Barkley, 1997; National Institutes of Health, 1994; Phelan, 1993).

Research Indicates

Although no one knows for sure what causes AD/HD, research tends to support a neurological basis for the disorder. Suspected causal factors include genetics and exposure to toxins during crucial stages of brain development. Sociocultural factors, such as diet and family dynamics, have been seen as influential in the manifestation of AD/HD, but not as causes of the disorder. (See Chapter 2, Causes; see also Barkley, 1997; Biederman & Faraone, 1996; National Institutes of Health, 1994.)

Misconception #2

AD/HD is a simple, singular disorder (Armstrong, 1995; Barkley, 1997).

Research Indicates

An entire chapter is devoted to comorbidity because it is a crucial factor impacting on the understanding of AD/HD. Most experts concur on the heterogeneity of the disorder and research indicates that many individuals with AD/HD have one or more other disorders. The frequency of comorbidity with AD/HD is highest with Conduct Disorder (CD) and Oppositional Defiance Disorder (ODD), followed by Learning Disabilities (LD), and then mood and anxiety disorders (Biederman, Newcorn, & Sprich, 1991). (See Chapter 3, Comorbidity; see also Barkley, 1997; Castellanos, 1997; Goldstein, 1997; Hallowell & Ratey, 1994a.)

Misconception #3

A medical diagnosis of AD/HD must come before classroom interventions are implemented (Damico & Augustine, 1995; Silver, 1992).

Research Indicates

Through increased knowledge and enhanced understanding, educators can be empowered to identify behaviors that are characteristic of AD/HD and to implement appropriate interventions. It is not necessary for a child to be tagged with a label for appropriate modifications to be made in the classroom. In addition, a collaborative team should work together to identify and meet the needs of AD/HD students. (See Chapter 4, Diagnosis; see also Damico & Augustine, 1995; Fowler, 1994; Phelan, 1993.)

Misconception #4

Medication is the preferred and only effective treatment used for children with AD/HD (Armstrong, 1995).

Research Indicates

Teachers can successfully approach AD/HD from an educational perspective, not a medical one. Recently, I heard a teacher say that she could not do anything until the child was put on medication—that had to be the first step. As a result of that kind of thinking, many children lose valuable instructional time waiting for help. Many nonmedical strategies can be utilized by educators to meet children's needs as they emerge.

For the 25–30% of children who do not improve on medication, it is imperative that alternative approaches be used. It is also important to recognize the fact that a response to a stimulant drug is not a confirmation of an AD/HD diagnosis. Many people, even those without AD/HD, improve in focusing and attending as a result of such medications (Damico & Augustine, 1995; Nemethy, 1997; National Institutes of Health, 1994). Children may be misdiagnosed with AD/HD if medicine is used as the first course of action, thus delaying a proper diagnosis (Nemethy, 1997).

Medication should not be used as an isolated treatment in most cases (Armstrong, 1995; Barkley, 1997; *Physicians' Desk Reference*, 1995). Although there are some contradictions, the majority of research findings have demonstrated the short-term benefits of stimulant medication for reducing hyperactivity, impulsivity, and aggression, but not for long-term or cognitive gains (see Chapter 5, Interventions; see also Armstrong, 1995; Barkley, 1997; Goldstein, 1997; Swanson et al., 1991). Some children who do not respond to medication alone show improvement when it is combined with other techniques.

Misconception #5

When it comes to interventions for students with AD/HD, one intervention is equally effective for all students with AD/HD (Phelan, 1993).

Research Indicates

Research demonstrates the complexity of AD/HD and the need to evaluate each student individually. Teachers must develop a fundamental understanding of the disorder to effectively select and implement interventions. Due to the uniqueness of each individual with AD/HD, no one technique is appropriate or effective for *all*. Most teachers, at least initially, want to know what they can do to meet the needs of their students with AD/HD. They expect a list of generic suggestions that can be indiscriminately applied. There are publications that provide such information. However, giving classroom strategies to teachers without first providing them with a basic understanding of the disorder is like putting a Band-Aid on an infected wound. It covers it up temporarily, but does not treat the underlying and pervasive problem. (See Chapter 2, Causes; Chapter 3, Comorbidity; Chapter 4, Diagnosis; Chapter 5, Interventions.)

COLLABORATION

AD/HD is described throughout this book as a disorder that occurs across settings. An individual with AD/HD does not have the option of being afflicted in one place and not in another. There are times when the situation contributes to the expression of the disorder. For example, if a child is extremely interested in a television show he may sit and watch quietly for a long period of time. The same child may fidget endlessly while doing a tedious homework assignment. However, by definition the symptoms must be present in two or more settings, such as school or work and home (see Appendix A). With that in mind, in order to help individuals with AD/HD, a coordinated effort to make appropriate accommodations across all environments should be pursued.

Many educators may be familiar with the term collaboration as it applies within a school setting among teachers. I am suggesting a much broader definition that would include all persons who have an impact on the life of the student with AD/HD. Parents, teachers, counselors, and health care providers need to work together toward the common goal of helping the individual with the disorder be successful (Churton, Cranston-Gingras, & Blair, 1998). The child with AD/HD should be paramount in that group, not only as a focus, but also as an active participant.

Successful collaboration is dependent on the establishment of a collaborative ethic (Churton, Cranston-Gingras, & Blair, 1998). When applied to AD/HD this refers to the belief that all parties should be involved in meeting the needs of the child with the disability. If teachers believe medication is the first and only answer, they will not be able to convince parents that teachers can meet the educational needs of the student. If parents feel alienated from the schools, they will seek professional help elsewhere. Positive, open-minded, and honest communication among all parties is essential for collaboration to work.

The Venn diagram in Figure 6.1 is a visual conceptualization of the collaborative interaction needed among team members. The student is the central focus and at the heart of the process. The arrows depict the ongoing, interactive communication between and among the parties. Each person

Figure 6.1
Interaction among Collaborative Team Members

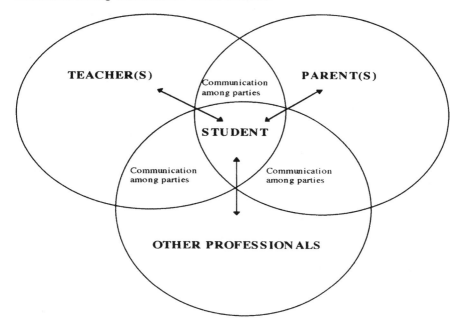

represented in the diagram is crucial to the success of the student with AD/HD, both individually and collectively as part of a team.

The Role of the Teacher

The teacher plays an important part in the development and success of the collaborative effort. This category could also include other school personnel that are involved with the student with AD/HD such as the principal, guidance counselor, and school psychologist. There are four ways in which the role of the educator can have a significant impact.

First and foremost, school personnel play a key part in establishing a positive rapport with parents. A teacher's ability to speak knowledgeably about AD/HD demonstrates to parents that the educator cares enough to be informed. The establishment of this perception is essential for open dialogue to begin and helps prevent the development of an adversarial attitude. This is the first step toward the creation of a collaborative ethic. It may also be necessary for the teacher to educate the parents on AD/HD as this may be their first encounter with the disorder (Snyder, 1997). Lending support during a difficult time when parents must come to terms with the fact that their child has a disability is an invaluable service.

The second way teachers can be helpful in developing collaborative relationships is by being knowledgeable about educational interventions that can be used effectively for AD/HD. All team members should brainstorm possible strategies to be implemented in the appropriate settings. The educator should be familiar with accommodations for use in school and specifically in the classroom. The parent may wish to pursue a medical evaluation at this time, in which case the teacher, as a member of the team, should be able to provide support and guidance in that regard.

Third, the teacher can develop and implement specific modifications and techniques based on the unique characteristics of each AD/HD student. The interventions ideally should be custom fit according to the student's AD/HD profile. In order to be successful in the selection of appropriate procedures, teachers should be knowledgeable about variables that have an impact on the particular student's academic and behavioral functioning. This would include such factors as comorbidity (co-occurrence) of AD/HD with other disorders and the diagnosed subtype (see Appendix A for *DSM-IV* definitions of AD/HD subtypes).

The fourth component of the teacher's role, which would be common to all team members, is the ongoing communication and monitoring of the effectiveness of accommodations. The collaborative process needs to be continuous, with evaluations and adjustments being made as necessary. There is no known "cure" for AD/HD, but there are accommodations that can be made to enrich the life of the individual with AD/HD and improve that individual's chances of experiencing success in school. To some extent, accommodations probably will be necessary throughout the school career of students with this disorder. The collaborative team is an ideal vehicle for providing this service, even if there is a change in membership over time.

The Role of the Parent

Oftentimes, parents feel as if the school is not responsive to their requests for assistance with the difficulties they are experiencing with a child with AD/HD. School personnel frequently perceive parents as uncooperative and difficult to deal with. To meet the needs of the student, both constituents need to get beyond the misperceptions and recognize each other's value. Parents have a significant role to play in the education of their children. They can be more effective in supporting the efforts of the school if they feel as if they are a part of the collaborative team.

Research shows that there is greater generalization of social skills across settings when parents are involved in the intervention (Frankel et al., 1997). In addition, coordinated programs between home and school can be quite effective (Barkley, 1990). Through tapping into the valuable resources available within a collaborative team, the chances of success on the part of a student with AD/HD are increased tremendously. Educators need to remember the vested interest that parents have in their children and view them as an asset.

The Role of the Student

It is essential that the individual with AD/HD be involved in and informed about most, if not all, aspects of the treatment. There are three aspects to the student's involvement. The first is awareness of the problem. Along with a label should come an explanation (Hallowell & Ratey, 1994b). Even a child as young as six years old is capable of comprehending a description if it is given in easily understandable terms. Making the person an active member of the team enhances the possibility of cooperation. Typically, educators, parents, and physicians administer a treatment to a child, making him the object or recipient of the procedure rather than a willing participant.

As the research has shown, individuals with AD/HD usually have difficulty with internal control. By involving the student in the process of intervention selection and through the use of self-management strategies, the focus can be redirected to one of internal rather than external control.

The student should know what to expect. This is particularly true with medication. The physician can get valuable feedback that can be used to make decisions regarding adjustments in dosage. Also, with understanding comes compliance (Turecki, 1997). Sometimes children will resist taking medication or spit it out when they think no one is looking. If they understand why they are taking the medication and how it may affect them, they become a part of the solution rather than a part of the problem.

Along with ownership of the disorder may come a sense of responsibility for one's actions (Barkley, 1997). Although it may not be within the individual's ability to completely control behavior, there are strategies that can be implemented by the student to ameliorate the effects. Empower the individual with AD/HD to take control of the disorder (Armstrong, 1995). Giving the child a means of dealing with the disability is far superior to doing it for the individual. Educators have the responsibility of providing students with whatever skills they need to be successful in life. For individuals with AD/HD this means helping them develop the ability to be as self-reliant as possible in implementing strategies to meet their own needs.

The Role of Other Professionals

Included in this category are such nonschool professionals as physicians, clinical counselors, and psychologists. Frequent communication and active participation on the collaborative team are significant functions of each of these members. It is especially important for the physician to monitor medication through other parties, if the student is receiving such treatment.

Counselors and psychologists can be an excellent source of feedback for treatment. Further discussion of these roles is beyond the scope of this book.

CHAPTER SUMMARY

Together we can make a difference. Approaching the challenges presented by students with AD/HD from a collaborative perspective increases the impact of our efforts tremendously. As the study done by Damico and Augustine (1995) illustrates, misperceptions and ineffective communication can create barriers between school personnel and parents of students with AD/HD. Educators are in the position to establish positive working relationships with families, other professionals, and individuals with the disorder that will aid all involved in meeting the challenges presented by AD/HD.

FINAL NOTE

Once when my son was two years old his baby sister was crying endlessly. I asked what we should do to help her and he replied, "Just love her, Mommy." Sometimes that is all we can do, but it means everything. My son's words have echoed in my mind many times since that day, and they have served me well as a guide with all of the children that have blessed my life. One of the most powerful interventions a teacher can have is a caring attitude. A genuine interest can be the driving force behind becoming knowledgeable and collaborating with others to make the world a better place for individuals with AD/HD.

REFERENCES

Armstrong, T. (1995). *The myth of the A.D.D. child*. New York: Penguin Books.

Barkley, R. A. (1990). *Attention-Deficit Hyperactivity Disorder: A handbook for diagnosis and treatment*. New York: Guilford Press.

Barkley, R. A. (1997). *ADHD and the nature of self-control*. New York: Guilford Press.

Biederman, J., & Faraone, S. (1996, Winter). On the brain: Studies on Attention Deficit Disorder. *The Harvard Mahoney Neuroscience Newsletter* [On-line], 5. Available: PsycINFO.

Biederman, J., Newcorn, J., & Sprich, S. (1991). Comorbidity of Attention Deficit Hyperactivity Disorder with Conduct, Depressive, Anxiety, and other disorders. *American Journal of Psychiatry, 148*(5), 564–577.

Castellanos, F. X. (1997). Approaching a scientific understanding of what happens in the brain in AD/HD. *Attention, 4*(1), 30–35.

Churton, M. W., Cranston-Gingras, A. M., & Blair, T. R. (1998). *Teaching children with diverse abilities*. Needham Heights, MA: Allyn and Bacon.

Damico, J. S., & Augustine, L. E. (1995). Social considerations in the labeling of students as Attention Deficit Hyperactivity Disordered. *Seminars in Speech and Language, 16*(4), 259–271.

Fowler, M. (1994, October). *Briefing paper: Attention-Deficit/Hyperactivity Disorder.* Washington, DC: National Information Center for Children and Youth with Disabilities (NICHCY).

Frankel, F., Myatt, R., Cantwell, D. P., & Feinberg, D. T. (1997, August). Parent-assisted transfer of children's social skills training: Effects on children with and without Attention-Deficit Hyperactivity Disorder. *Journal of American Academy of Child and Adolescent Psychiatry, 36*(8), 1056–1064.

Goldstein, S. (1997). *Managing learning and attention disorders in late adolescence and adulthood.* New York: Wiley.

Hallowell, E., & Ratey, J. (1994a). *Answers to distraction.* New York: Random House.

Hallowell, E., & Ratey, J. (1994b). *Driven to distraction.* New York: Random House.

National Institutes of Health. (1994). *Attention Deficit Hyperactivity Disorder.* Washington, DC: Author.

Nemethy, M. (1997, February). Attention Deficit/Hyperactivity Disorder. *Advance for Nurse Practitioners,* 22–29.

Phelan, T. (1993). *All about Attention Deficit Disorder.* Glen Ellyn, IL: Child Management, Inc.

Physicians' desk reference (49th ed.). (1995). Montvale, NJ: Medical Economics Data Production Company.

Silver, L. (1992). *Attention-Deficit Hyperactivity Disorder.* Washington, DC: American Pediatric Press.

Snyder, M. (1997). Parents' perceptions of school services for children with ADD: Communication is the key. *Attention, 4*(1), 10–12.

Swanson, J. M., Cantwell, D., Lerner, M., McBurnett, K., & Hanna, G. (1991). Effects of stimulant medication on children with ADHD. *Journal of Learning Disabilities, 24*(4), 219–230.

Turecki, S. (1997, November). *Practical psychopharmacology for children.* Paper presented at the Nurse Practiner Associates for Continuing Education (NPACE), Boston, MA.

Appendix A

Definition of Attention Deficit/Hyperactivity Disorder

AD/HD is defined as:

A. Either (1) or (2):

(1) Six (or more) of the following symptoms of *inattention* have persisted for at least six months to a degree that is maladaptive and inconsistent with developmental level:

Inattention

(a) often fails to give close attention to details or makes careless mistakes in schoolwork, work, or other activities

(b) often has difficulty in sustaining attention in tasks or play activities

(c) often does not seem to listen when spoken to directly

(d) often does not follow through on instructions and fails to finish schoolwork, chores, or duties in the workplace (not due to oppositional behavior or failure to understand instructions)

(e) often has difficulty organizing tasks or activities

(f) often avoids, dislikes, or is reluctant to engage in tasks that require sustained mental effort (such as schoolwork or homework)

(g) often loses things necessary for tasks or activities

(h) often is easily distracted by extraneous stimuli

(i) often is forgetful in daily activities

(2) Six (or more) of the following symptoms of *hyperactivity-impulsivity* have persisted for at least six months to a degree that is maladaptive and inconsistent with developmental level:

Hyperactivity

(a) often fidgets with hands or feet or squirms in seat

(b) often leaves seat in classroom or in other situations in which remaining seated is expected

(c) often runs about or climbs excessively in situations in which it is inappropriate (in adolescents or adults, may be limited to subjective feelings of restlessness)

(d) often has difficulty playing or engaging in leisure activities quietly

(e) often is "on the go" or often acts as if "driven by a motor"

(f) often talks excessively

(g) often blurts out answers before questions have been completed

(h) often has difficulty awaiting turn

(i) often interrupts or intrudes on others (e.g., butts into conversations or games)

B. Some hyperactive-impulsive symptoms that caused impairment were present before age seven years.

C. Some impairment from the symptoms is present in two or more settings (e.g., at school [or work] and at home).

D. There must be clear evidence of clinically significant impairment in social, academic, or occupational functioning.

E. The symptoms do not occur exclusively during the course of a Pervasive Developmental Disorder, Schizophrenia, or other Psychotic Disorder and are not better accounted for by another mental disorder (e.g., Mood Disorder, Anxiety Disorder, Dissociative Disorder, or Personality Disorder).

Code based on type:

   314.01 Attention-Deficit/Hyperactivity Disorder, Combined Type: if both Criteria A1 and A2 are met for the past 6 months

   314.00 Attention-Deficit/Hyperactivity Disorder, Predominantly Inattentive Type: if Criterion A1 is met but Criterion A2 is not met for the past 6 months

   314.01 Attention-Deficit/Hyperactivity Disorder, Predominantly Hyperactive-Impulsive Type: if Criterion A2 is met but Criterion A1 is not met for the past 6 months

NOTE

From American Psychiatric Association. (1994). *Diagnostic Statistical Manual of Mental Disorders* (4th ed.) (pp.83–85). Washington, DC: Author. Reprinted with permission from the *Diagnostic and Statistical Manual of Mental Disorders*, Fourth Edition. Copyright 1994 American Psychiatric Association.

Appendix B

Evaluation Criteria for Article Selection

Definition of Headings

I. Reputation of Journal: (X) = a journal that referees submissions prior to approval for publication.

II. Date of Publication

III. Relevance of the Study to Educators:

(C) = enhances teacher's communication with others

(T) = has direct application to teaching

(D) = facilitates decision making

(U) = contributes to a basic understanding of AD/HD

IV. Representative of a Body of Literature: (X) = research is cited in the article that supports and reflects the general findings of the literature. The number represents items in the reference list.

Definition of Terms

Experimental: a study in which the subjects are randomly assigned to categories and involving one or more manipulated variables

Quasi-experimental: a study in which at least one variable is manipulated but subjects are not randomly assigned to groups

Nonexperimental: a study in which there is no manipulation of variables and no randomization of assignment of subjects

NOTE

The definition of terms are from *Measurement, Design, and Analysis: An Integrated Approach* by J. E. Pedhazur and L. P. Schmelkin, 1991, Hillsdale, NJ: Lawrence Erlbaum.

Title of the Article	Reputation of Journal	Date of Publication	Relevance to Educators	Represents a Body of Literature (# References)
Chapter 2: Causes of AD/HD				
1. Evidence of Familial Association between Attention Deficit Disorder and Major Affective Disorders (Nonexperimental)	X	1991	U, C	X (62)
2. Further Evidence for Family-Genetic Risk Factors in AD/HD (Nonexperimental)	X	1992	U, C	X (85)
3. Genetic Heterogeneity in AD/HD: Gender, Psychiatric Comorbidity, and Maternal AD/HD (Nonexperimental)	X	1995	U, C	X (68)
4. AD/HD in People with Generalized Resistance to Thyroid Hormone (Nonexperimental)	X	1993	U, C	X (30)
5. Learning Disorders and the Thyroid (Letter to the Editor)	N/A	1996	U	N/A
6. Etiology of AD/HD: Nature or Nurture? (Letter to the Editor)	N/A	1996	U	N/A
7. Is Maternal Smoking during Pregnancy a Risk Factor for AD/HD in Children? (Nonexperimental)	X	1996	U, C	X (43)

8. Psychiatric Sequelae of Low-birth-weight at 6 Years of Age (Nonexperimental)	X	1996	U, C	X (45)
9. Psychiatric Outcomes in Low-birth-weight Children at Age 6 Years: Relation to Neonatal Cranial Ultrasound Abnormalities (Nonexperimental)	X	1997	U, C	X (103)
10. Association of Attention-Deficit Disorder and the Dopamine Transporter Gene (Nonexperimental)	X	1995	U, C	X (34)
11. Essential Fatty Acid Metabolism in Boys with AD/HD (Nonexperimental)	X	1995	U, C	X (46)
12. Relationship between Serum Free Fatty Acids and Zinc, and AD/HD (Nonexperimental)	X	1996	U, C	X (16)
13. Quantitative Morphology of the Caudate Nucleus in AD/HD (Nonexperimental)	X	1994	U, C	X (49)
14. Quantitative Brain Magnetic Resonance Imaging in AD/HD (Nonexperimental)	X	1996	U, C	X (113)
15. Gender Differences in ADHD (Meta-analysis)	X	1997	U, C, D	X (30)

Chapter 3: Comorbidity of AD/HD with Other Disorders				
1. Comorbidity in AD/HD: Implications for Research, Practice, and *DSM-V* (Review of literature on AD/HD for past 15 years)	X	1997	U, C, D	X (69)
2. Comorbidity of AD/HD with Conduct, Depressive, Anxiety, and Other Disorders (Systematic Search of Literature)	X	1991	U, C, D	X (118)
3. A Prospective 4-Year Follow-up Study of Attention-Deficit Hyperactivity and Related Disorders (Nonexperimental)	X	1996	U, C, D	X (55)
4. Patterns of Comorbidity Associated with Subtypes of AD/HD among 6- to 12-Year-Old Children (Nonexperimental)	X	1997	U, C, D	X (53)
5. Psychiatric Comorbidity among Referred Juveniles with Major Depression: Fact or Artifact? (Nonexperimental)	X	1995	U, C, D	X (57)
6. Mania-like Symptoms Suggestive of Childhood-onset Bipolar Disorder in Clinically Referred Children (Nonexperimental)	X	1995	U, C, D	X (51)

7. Parent	X	1996	U, C, D, T	X
Characteristics and				(41)
Parent-child				
Interactions in				
Families with				
Nonproblem				
Children and				
AD/HD Children				
with Higher and				
Lower Levels of				
Oppositional-defiant				
Behavior				
(Nonexperimental)				
8. Coincidence of	X	1991	C, U	X
Attention Deficit				(47)
Disorder and Atopic				
Disorders in				
Children: Empirical				
Findings and				
Hypothetical				
Background				
(Nonexperimental)				
9. Prevalence of	X	1996	C, D	X
AD/HD and				(61)
Comorbid Disorders				
among Elementary				
School Children				
Screened for				
Disruptive Behavior				
(Nonexperimental)				

Chapter 4: Diagnosis of AD/HD

1. A Prospective Four-	X	1996	C, D	X
year Follow-up				(43)
Study of Children at				
Risk for AD/HD:				
Psychiatric,				
Neuropsychological,				
and Psychosocial				
Outcome				
(Nonexperimental)				
2. Toward a New	X	1996	U, C, D	X
Psychometric				(42)
Definition of Social				
Disability in				
Children with				
AD/HD				
(Nonexperimental)				

3. Social Considerations in the Labeling of Students as Attention Deficit Hyperactive Disordered (Ethnography)	X	1995	U, C, D	X (36)
4. Methodological Differences in the Diagnosis of AD/HD: Impact on Prevalence (Nonexperimental)	X	1994	U, C, D	X (37)
5. Comparison of Diagnostic Criteria for AD/HD in a County-wide Sample (Nonexperimental)	X	1996	U, C	X (23)
6. Validity of *DSM-IV* ADHD Predominantly Inattentive and Combined Types: Relationship to Previous *DSM* Diagnoses/Subtype Differences (Nonexperimental)	X	1996	U, C, D	X (49)
7. Prediction of Group Membership in Developmental Dyslexia, AD/HD, and Normal Controls Using Brain Morphometric Analysis of Magnetic Resonance Imaging (Nonexperimental)	X	1996	U	X (19)
8. Quantitative EEG Differences in a Nonclinical Sample of Children with ADHD and Undifferentiated ADD (Nonexperimental)	X	1996	U	X (35)

9. Is Continuous Performance Task a Valuable Research Tool for Use with Children with AD/HD? (Nonexperimental)	X	1993	U	X (38)

Chapter 5: Interventions for AD/HD

1. Behavioral Treatment of AD/HD in the Classroom (Quasi-experimental)	X	1992	U, C, D, T	X (25)
2. Promoting Academic Performance in Inattentive Children (Quasi-experimental)	X	1995	U, C, D, T	X (19)
3. Effects of Reward and Response Cost on Performance and Motivation in ADHD (Quasi-experimental)	X	In Press	U, C, D, T	X (27)
4. Methylphenidate and Attentional Training (Nonexperimental)	X	1996	U, C, D, T	X (47)
5. Initiating and Fading Self-management Interventions to Increase Math Fluency in General Education Classes (Nonexperimental)	X	1998	U, C, D, T	X (59)
6. Attentional Focus of Students with Hyperactivity during a Word-search Task (Quasi-experimental)	X	In Press	U, D	X (34)
7. Computer-assisted Cognitive Training for AD/HD (Case Study)	X	1996	U, C, D, T	X (23)

8. Structured Tasks: Effects on Activity and Performance of Hyperactive and Comparison Children (Quasi-experimental)	X	1985	U, C, D, T	X (30)
9. Effects of Color Stimulation and Information on the Copying Performance of Attention-Problem Adolescents (Quasi-experimental)	X	1985	U, C, D, T	X (27)
10. Attentional Cuing in Spelling Tasks for Hyperactive and Comparison Regular Classroom Children (Quasi-experimental)	X	1989	U, C, D, T	X (22)
11. Peer Tutoring Effects on the Classroom Performance of Children with AD/HD (Case Study)	X	1993	U, C, D, T	X (22)
12. The Effects of School-based Interventions for ADHD (Meta-analysis)	X	1997	U, C, D, T	X (80)
13. Who Are the Children with ADHD? (School-based Survey)	X	1994	U, C, D, T	X (89)
14. Parent-assisted Transfer of Children's Social Skills Training: Effects on Children with and without AD/HD (Quasi-experimental)	X	1997	U, C, D, T	X (64)

15. Long-term Stimulant Treatment of Children with ADHD Symptoms (Experimental)	X	1997	U, C	X (34)
16. Classroom Academic Performance: Improvement with Both Methylphenidate and Dextro-amphetamine (Experimental)	X	1993	U, C	X (58)

Appendix C

Definition of Conduct Disorder

Conduct Disorder is defined as:

1. Serious violation of rules and societal norms
2. Presence of three or more of the following characteristics in the past 12 months:
   - threatens/causes physical harm to other people or animals
   - destroys property of others including setting fires to cause damage
   - lies, steals
   - breaks rules: truancy, runs away from home, violates curfews

NOTE

From American Psychiatric Association. (1994). *Diagnostic Statistical Manual of Mental Disorders* (4th ed.). Washington, DC: Author.

Definition of Oppositional Defiant Disorder

According to *DSM-IV*, Oppositional Defiant Disorder is defined as:

1. Less serious behaviors than exhibited with Conduct Disorder, without aggression toward people and animals
2. More defiance toward authority figures
3. Four or more of the following characteristics present for the previous six months:
   - frequently loses temper
   - argumentative with adults
   - defies authority
   - deliberately annoying to others
   - projects blame onto others
   - frequently angry, or spiteful
   - easily annoyed by others

If the individual qualifies for the diagnosis of Conduct Disorder and Oppositional Defiant Disorder, only the diagnosis of Conduct Disorder is applied.

NOTE

From American Psychiatric Association. (1994). *Diagnostic Statistical Manual of Mental Disorders* (4th ed.). Washington, DC: Author.

Synopses of *Diagnostic and Statistical Manual of Mental Disorders* Definitions of AD/HD by Edition (*DSM-II, DSM-III, and DSM-III-R*)

DSM-II (APA, 1968)—**Hyperkinetic reaction of childhood (or adolescence):** The definition focuses on hyperactivity, impulsivity, restlessness, and short attention span. The disorder is reported as occurring in early childhood and diminishing in adolescence.

DSM-III (APA, 1980)—**Attention Deficit Disorder with or without Hyperactivity:** The diagnostic criteria include the presence of symptoms of inattention, impulsivity, and hyperactivity. Special regard is given to situational differences, with preference given to teacher reports over parent reports. The age of onset is specified as before age seven, with at least six months duration. Conditions not included are Schizophrenia, Affective Disorder, or Severe or Profound Mental Retardation.

DSM-III-R (APA, 1987)—**Attention-Deficit Hyperactivity Disorder in Children:** The criteria include 14 items of which at least 8 must be present before seven years of age. No subtypes are recognized and ADD without hyperactivity is classified as Undifferentiated ADD (UADD). A diagnosis of Pervasive Developmental Disorder would exclude an individual from the category of ADD.

Appendix F

Self-management Techniques Resource List

Armstrong, T. (1995). *The myth of the A.D.D. child*. New York: Penguin Books.

Bash, M. S., & Camp, B. (1985). *Think aloud: Increasing social and cognitive skills—A problem solving program for children*. Champaign, IL: Research Press.

Block, D., & Merritt, J. (1993). *Positive self-talk for children*. New York: Bantam.

DeBrueys, M. T. (Project Coordinator). (1986). *125 ways to be a better student: A program for study skills success*. Moline, IL: LinguiSystems.

Goldstein, S., & Goldstein, M. (1990). *Managing attention disorders in children*. New York: Wiley.

Gordon, M. (1987). *The Attention Training System (ATS)*. New York: Gordon Systems.

Isaacs, S., & Richie W. (1991). *I think I can, I know I can: Using self-talk to help raise confident, secure kids*. New York: St. Martin's.

Psychological Corporation/Harcourt Brace Jovanovich. (1991). THINKable Rehabilitation System [Computer program]. San Antonio, TX: Author (555 Academic Court, San Antonio, TX 78204).

Sanford, J. A., & Browne, R. J. (1988). Captain's Log [Computer software]. Richmond, VA: Braintrain.

Appendix G

Social Skills Resource List

Armstrong, T. (1995). *The myth of the A.D.D. child*. New York: Penguin Books.

Domash, L., & Sachs, J. (1994). *Wanna be my friend? How to strengthen your child's social skills*. New York: Hearst.

Elardo, P., & Cooper, M. (1977). *AWARE: Activities for social development*. Menlo Park, CA: Addision-Wesley.

Elksnin, L. K. (1996). Promoting success in the mainstream: Collaborative social skills instruction. *Reading & Writing Quarterly, 12*, 345–350.

Elksnin, L. K., & Elksnin, N. (1998). Teaching social skills to students with learning and behavior problems. *Intervention in School and Clinic, 33*(3), 131–140.

Goldstein, A. P., Sprafkin, R. P., Gershaw, N. J., & Klein, P. (1980). *Skill-streaming the adolescent: A structured learning approach to teaching prosocial skills*. Champaign, IL: Research Press.

Goldstein, S., & Goldstein, M. (1990). *Managing attention disorders in children*. New York: Wiley.

Hazel, J. S., Schumaker, J. B., Sherman, J. A., & Sheldon, J. (1995). *ASSET: A social skills program for adolescents* (2nd ed.). Champaign, IL: Research Press.

Jones, R. N., Sheridan, S. M., & Binns, W. R. (1993). Schoolwide social skills training: Providing preventive services to students at-risk. *School Psychology Quarterly, 8*, 57–80.

McGinnis, E., Goldstein, A. P., Sprafkin, R. P., & Gershaw, N. J. (1984). *Skill-streaming the elementary school child: A guide for teaching prosocial skills*. Champaign, IL: Research Press.

Stephens, T. M. (1992). *Social skills in the classroom* (2nd ed.). Odessa, FL: Psychological Assessment Resources.

Walker, H. M., Todis, B., Holmes, D., & Horton, G. (1988). *The Walker social skills curriculum: The ACCESS Program*. Austin, TX: Pro-Ed.

Medications Used in the Treatment of AD/HD

Medication	Dosage	Side Effects
Psychostimulants		
Methylphenidate (Ritalin) tablet * 3–4 hrs.	• 5 mg, 10 mg, 20 mg (not for children under six yrs. of age) • Time to reach peak effect in children— 1.9 hrs.	• loss of appetite • weight loss • insomnia, tics • headaches • nervousness • abdominal pain • controlled substance with potential for abuse
Sustained release tablet * 6–8 hrs.	• 20 mg (not for children under six yrs. of age)	
Dextroamphetamine (Dexedrine) tablet * 4–6 hrs.	• 5 mg (not for children under three yrs. of age)	• appetite suppression • compulsive behaviors • insomnia
Sustained release capsule * 8–12 hrs.	• 5 mg, 10 mg, 15 mg	• irritability • controlled substance with potential for abuse
Dextroamphetamine Sulfate (Adderall)	• 10 mg, 20 mg (not for children under three yrs. of age)	• palpitations • elevated blood pressure • insomnia, tics • euphoria, dizziness • headaches, nausea • weight loss • dry mouth • restlessness • controlled substance with potential for abuse

| Pemoline (Cylert) tablet
* 12–24 hrs.
chewable | • 18.75 mg, 37.5 mg,
75 mg
• 37.5 mg | • 3 to 4 weeks to work
• insomnia, headaches
• temporary weight loss
• drowsiness, dizziness
• irritability, tics
• stomach aches
• rare reports of liver
problems
• not a controlled
substance, low potential
for abuse |

Antidepressants

| Imipramine (Tofranil)
tablets | • 10 mg, 25 mg, 50
mg (not to exceed
2.5 mg in children) | • ECG changes
• sensitivity to sunlight
• may take up to 3 weeks
to work |

* = Length of Action   ECG = electrocardiogram
Note: The data for length of action are from "Medication: Your questions answered," by W.
    Coleman, 1994, *Challenge, 8*, p.4.
Note: From *Physicians' Desk Reference*, 49th ed., 1995.

Appendix I

Guidelines for Educational Interventions

- Place the student with teachers who are positive, upbeat, highly organized problem-solvers.
- Provide the student with a structured and predictable environment.
- Modify the curriculum.
- For excessive activity:
  1. Channel activity into acceptable avenues.
  2. Use activity as a reward.
  3. Use active responses in instruction.
- For inability to wait:
  1. Give the child substitute verbal and motor responses to make while waiting.
  2. When possible, allow daydreaming and planning while the child waits.
  3. Suggest alternative behaviors (e.g., line leader, paper passer).
- For failure to sustain attention to routine tasks and activities:
  1. Decrease the length of the task.
  2. Make tasks interesting.
- For noncompliance and failure to complete tasks:
  1. Generally increase the choice and specific interest of tasks for the child.
  2. Make sure tasks fit within the student's learning abilities and preferred response style.
- For difficulty at the beginning of tasks:
  1. Increase the structure of tasks and highlight important parts.
- For completing assignments on time:

1. Increase the student's use of lists and assignment organizers (notebooks, folders), write assignments on the board and make sure the student has copied them.

2. Establish routines to place and retrieve commonly used objects such as books, assignments, and clothes.

3. Teach the student that, upon leaving one place for another, he or she will self-question, "Do I have everything I need?"

NOTE

From *National Information Center for Children and Youth with Disabilities (NICHCY) Briefing Paper* by M. Fowler, 1994, Washington, DC: National Information Center for Children and Youth with Disabilities. Copyright free information.

Appendix J

Additional Intervention Strategies Resource List

Armstrong, T. (1995). *The myth of the A.D.D. child*. New York: Penguin Books.

Fowler, M. (1994, October). *Briefing paper: Attention-Deficit/Hyperactivity Disorder*. Washington, DC: National Information Center for Children and Youth with Disabilities (NICHCY).

Goldstein, S., & Goldstein, M. (1990). *Managing attention disorders in children*. New York: Wiley.

Shinsky, E. J. (1996). *Students with special needs: A resource guide for teachers*. Lansing, MI: Shinsky Seminars, Inc.

Virginia Department of Education. (n.d.). *Attention Deficit Hyperactivity Disorder and the schools* (Task Force Report). Richmond, VA: Author.

Index

academic interventions, 64, 78, 83
allergies, 32, 41, 42, 45
antidepressants, 34. *See also* medication
antisocial, 11–13, 33, 37
Antisocial Personality Disorder, 12, 34
Anxiety Disorder, 16, 31, 34–36, 39, 44
ATS (Attention Training System), 67, 70, 91
Attention Training System (ATS), 67, 70, 91
autism, 11

Bandura, Albert, 71
behavior modification, 64–66, 72
behavior rating scales, 16, 18, 19
Bipolar Disorder, 10, 31, 37, 39, 40, 44
brain damage, 17
brain differences, 2, 16, 17, 56, 57
brain research, 3
brain theory, 3

CD (Conduct Disorder), 11, 13, 25, 31, 33–36, 37, 38, 39, 43, 44, 45, 55, 102
cognitive strategies, 64

collaboration, 53, 60, 101, 104
Conduct Disorder (CD), 11, 13, 25, 31, 33–36, 37, 38, 39, 43, 44, 45, 55, 102
continuous performance task (CPT), 56, 57, 59
CPT (continuous performance task), 56, 57, 59

Dexedrine, 70, 86, 88, 89
Diagnostic and Statistical Manual of Mental Disorders (DSM), 2, 31, 33, 38, 43, 44, 48, 49, 50, 53–60, 70, 106; *DSM-III*, 55, 56; *DSM-III-R*, 50, 55, 56, 58, 59, 70; *DSM-IV*, 2, 31, 33, 38, 43, 44, 48, 49, 54–60, 106
disruptive behavior, 42, 43, 45, 58, 76, 81, 90
dopamine, 18, 19, 26, 41

EEG (electroencephalogram), 49, 56, 57, 58
electroencephalogram (EEG), 49, 56, 57, 58
environmental factors, 1–3, 10–14, 24, 34, 52, 53

About the Author

CAROL R. LENSCH is Assistant Professor in the Education Department at Hollins University, Virginia.

ISBN 0-89789-700-5

90000>

EAN

9 780897 897006

HARDCOVER BAR CODE